THE PRESIDENT'S SERIES
IN ARKANSAS AND REGIONAL STUDIES

honoring Dr. James E. Martin
whose courage and vision made possible
the establishment of
The University of Arkansas Press

volume one

Vinegar Pie and Chicken Bread

The Jackson family about 1896. Clockwise from upper left are
Lizzie, Sue, James Coose (Lizzie's husband), W. T., Carrie,
Nannie, and "Stonewall." (Courtesy of Virginia Sue Meade)

VINEGAR PIE
AND CHICKEN BREAD

A Woman's Diary of Life

in the Rural South,

1890–1891

Edited with an Introduction
by Margaret Jones Bolsterli

The University of Arkansas Press
Fayetteville
1982

Copyright © 1982 by
Board of Trustees of the University of Arkansas
The University of Arkansas Press, Fayetteville, Arkansas 72701
Library of Congress Catalog Card Number 82–4922
Printed and bound in the United States of America

Library of Congress Cataloging in Publication Data
Jackson, Nannie Stillwell.
Vinegar Pie and Chicken Bread
Bibliography: p.
1. Jackson, Nannie Stillwell. 2. Desha County (Ark.)
—Social life and customs. 3. Country life—Arkansas
—Desha County. 4. Country life—Southern States.
5. Desha County (Ark.)—Biography. I. Bolsterli,
Margaret Jones. II. Title.
F417.D4J334   976.7'85051'0924 [B]   82–4922
ISBN 0–938626–10–8   AACR2

For the memory of my parents,
whose stories taught me who I am.
And for Grover, Pauline,
Jodie, Ted, and Bob.

Contents

Preface, xi

Introduction, 1

The Diary, 23

Glossary, 101

Bibliography, 103

Index, 105

Preface

In 1978, while looking for original material about Arkansas for use in a research course I was teaching at the university, I heard about a diary kept by Nannie Stillwell Jackson in Watson, a small town in Desha County, in 1890. I was immediately interested in this manuscript because my mother, as a very young schoolteacher, had boarded with Mrs. Jackson about 1907, so many of the names mentioned in it were familiar to me. However, since it soon became obvious that this diary had much more to offer of historical value than either the topicality that held my personal interest or its usefulness as a research exercise for my students, I decided to make it accessible to both historians and laymen interested in reading a detailed account of routine existence in the rural South at the end of the nineteenth century.

From 11 June 1890 to 15 April 1891, Nannie Stillwell Jackson kept a diary with pencils in a small ledger, twenty by thirteen centimeters in size. Mrs. Jackson's writing is neat and legible, but the pages at the beginning and end of the ledger have deteriorated so badly that familiarity with local names was frequently my salvation in deciphering meaning. No pages are missing, so missing entries indicate days on which Mrs. Jackson did not write. There is some evidence that this ledger is only a segment of a diary that Mrs. Jackson kept for many years. Elderly people in Watson remember referring to entries made in 1888 several years ago while searching for sources of local church history. The manuscript is now in Special Collections at the University of Arkansas Library in Fayetteville.

In order to preserve the flavor of the document, I have made an exact copy. It seemed to me that correcting the punctuation to make the material more readable would have meant changing it to something that Mrs. Jackson did not write, that the inconvenience of having to sort out occasionally erratic punctuation would be compensated by retaining the feel of the diary. This was, after all, a private record kept for her use alone and therefore one in which she did not have to pay much attention to punctuation and spelling. It is worth noting that her ability to make her meaning clear was recognized by her being called upon to write letters for neighbors who could not do it for themselves. For guidance she had a copy of *The American Fashionable Letter Writer*, containing samples "on Business, Courtship, Marriage, Relationship, Friendship, and Valentine with forms of Complimentary Cards." Judging from surviving letters written to Mrs. Jackson, her approach to her correspondence was as methodical as that to her diary. She answered letters immediately, noting her date of reply on each one.

I have made every effort to identify all the people mentioned in this diary, a task made more difficult than it would have been had the diary been kept either ten years earlier or later by the 1890 census rolls for this part of the country having been destroyed. Lacking the 1890 records, I had to rely on those for 1880 and 1900, which were useful but not conclusive since even in a society as static as this one some people inevitably moved away and many died in that span of twenty years. I have consulted the little published material available in biographical memoirs and newspapers about early residents of Desha County. While most of the people who pass across Mrs. Jackson's pages do not often turn up in histories, a few, including the Jacksons, managed to scrape together the fee charged for inclusion in *Biographical and Historical Memoirs of Southern Arkansas*. The *Programs of the Desha County Historical Society* were extremely useful, as was an unpublished history of Watson compiled by Jim Merritt of McGehee, Arkansas. To avoid useless interruption I have provided notes only for people about whom I could offer some kind of information. I have included also a glossary of terms that might otherwise confuse a contemporary reader.

In expressing gratitude to the many people who helped

with this project, I must first thank Ila Marie Preddy for her generosity in lending this manuscript and then donating it to the library. Virginia Sue Meade, Nannie Stillwell Jackson's granddaughter, gave invaluable help by sharing her memories and by allowing unrestricted use of family records, letters, and photographs. Bessie Morgan, Hattie Hundley, and Joe Stroud helped me better understand the time in which this diary was kept. Mae Willis and the late C. D. Dupree kindly allowed me to examine their collections of photographs for illustrations. Grover Jones of Dumas and Pauline Lloyd of Watson gave me access to the Jones family papers and put me up while I was doing research in Desha County. Without the assistance of James O. Ross, Desha County Tax Assessor, I would not have located the appropriate tax records so easily, and Kathleen Siever and Donna McGraw helped with the search in the office of the Desha County Department of Education. Jim Merritt generously lent his unpublished history of Watson. Ethel Simpson and Marcus Woodward of Special Collections at the University of Arkansas Library deserve special recognition for their diligence in helping me find useful material.

I want to thank the Arkansas Endowment for the Humanities and the University of Arkansas for the matching grant that allowed me to take time off from teaching to finish this work. And finally, I wish to express my deep gratitude to Willard B. Gatewood, Jr., Olivia Sordo, Gwen Kirkpatrick, and Diane Blair for their continual encouragement and specific suggestions for improving this manuscript.

M. J. B.
March 1982
Fayetteville, Arkansas

Fannie Morgan and two children about 1895.
(Courtesy of Virginia Sue Meade)

Fannie Morgan and two young women in 1914.
(Courtesy of Virginia Sue Meade)

Friday June 27th 1890
clear & warming cloudy
up late this evening but
it did not rain any here
Lizzie washed to day & was
until 3 oclock getting done
she washed her doll clothes
& I made starch & she &
Sue starched their doll
clothes Sue washed her
doll clothes tuesday I did
some patching for Fannie
& day & took it & her
she washed again yester
day & ironed up everything
to day I also took the 2 bunch
es of moss & set out in a
box for her, when I came
back Mr. Jackson got
mad at me for going up
there 3 times this evening
said I went to talk about
him, he got mad & said I
was working for nothing
but to get him & Mr
Morgan in a row, & to
make trouble between
them & I just talk to
Fannie & tell her my
troubles because it seems
to help me to bear it better
when she knows about it
& I shall tell her whenever
I feel like it — he accuses
me of mean things because
_____ _____ to _____ _____

The diary entry for 27 June 1890.
(Courtesy of University of Arkansas Library)

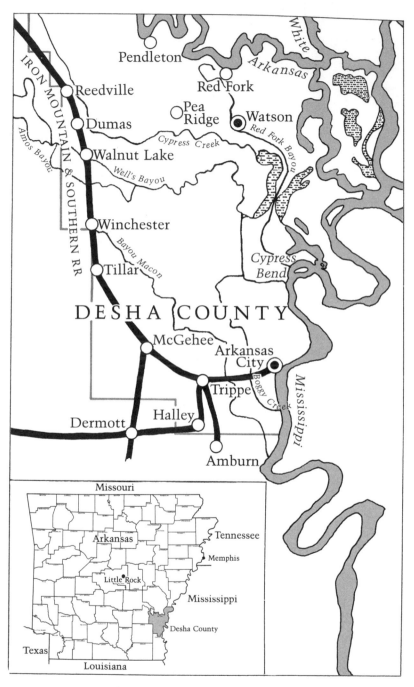

Desha County, as it appeared in 1890.

Introduction

Ironically, the value of this document lies in its tedium. While most diaries are preserved either because they were kept by influential people or record events of unusual times, Nannie Stillwell Jackson's record was kept by a "nobody" in a place and time where virtually nothing was happening. Since for lack of anything exciting she wrote about the details of the everyday existence of her houschold and her friends, she left a record of the way ordinary people in the rural South coped without hospitals, funeral homes, telephones, railroads, dependable roads, electricity, running water, automobiles, or any labor-saving devices. As a record of the endurance that must be grasped if we are to understand our national past, it is part of that testimony which Thomas R. Frazier, in his collection of essays of the same name, defined as the "underside of history." An especially valuable part of that underside lies in Mrs. Jackson's account of keeping house and "visiting" with her women friends, as this illuminates an aspect of women's experience about which very little is known. Until recently there has been so little interest in women's lives that few records have been kept. Another valuable aspect of this underside that Mrs. Jackson exposes is the stifling, intellectually empty, mind-deadening quality of life in nineteenth-century rural America, which helps account for the provincial attitudes still prevalent in some areas today. The traditional limitations of vision in such places are better understood in the context of their background in a world like Mrs. Jackson's, which seems to stop, both literally and figuratively, at the edge of the woods surrounding Watson.

In addition, there is evidence here of various patterns of community life. We are permitted to observe a support system among women which reveals a women's culture that coexisted with both a men's culture and another shared by

1

men and women. Relations between blacks and whites are illuminated by Mrs. Jackson's account of her association with black people in Watson, and the paths of cultural exchange between the races can be seen in the types of communication between them. Furthermore, a highly developed sense of community responsibility is evident in the way individuals step forward to care for each other during crises. Along with these glimpses of community structures, this diary provides us with the detailed context of Southern novels set in an era that is growing distant at a staggering pace as technology rapidly changes the face of the rural South. In this connection, one thinks first of Addie Bundren in William Faulkner's *As I Lay Dying*, who had much in common with Nannie Jackson, and then of the Beecham family in Eudora Welty's *Losing Battles*, whose battles were similar to those of the Jackson family.

Finally, although details about things like food make it plain that this is a *Southern* community, Mrs. Jackson's documentation of the daily routine in Watson takes on broader implications when the representative nature of this existence is taken into account, for most American farmers of that time had about the same amount of land as the Jacksons. According to the census tabulations for 1890, the average size of farms in the South Central region, which includes Arkansas, was 144 acres; the average size of farms in the United States was 137 acres. The Jacksons owned 140 acres. Furthermore, there were 4,564,641 farms in the United States in 1890, and only 450 towns with population of more than 8,000 inhabitants.[1] (Although four of these towns were in Arkansas, it is unlikely that Mrs. Jackson ever visited any of them, with the possible exception of Pine Bluff, some fifty miles away.) So there were literally millions of people in this country living much as the Jacksons lived. on the edge of poverty but with a place in the community, however precarious, that allowed them a certain measure of dignity. The

---

1. *Abstract of the Eleventh Census*, p. 60.

gravity of their situation can be appreciated when two facts are comprehended: the price of cotton in 1890–1893 averaged 7.8 cents a pound, a figure below the level at which a profit could be made,[2] and the Jacksons had to borrow against the expectations of each crop the money to make it with. So they were caught in that terrible pull between the fall of cotton prices and the lien system of crop financing that gave such impetus to the Populist movement in the South. From Mrs. Jackson's account, one can almost feel what it was like to be a small farmer on a treadmill who could in good years barely make ends meet and in bad years might go under and lose the land itself. In fact, the diary is, in its way, as poignant a witness to this class of Southern farmer as the portraits by James Agee and Walker Evans in *Let Us Now Praise Famous Men* are to sharecroppers during the Great Depression.

The reader must be prepared to accept the sometimes tedious nature of reading about such a tedious existence. It is a measure of the limitations of that life that Mrs. Jackson's days could be so brightened by the gift of a dish of greens or a pat of butter and a short visit. The fact of a hen abandoning her nest was worth recording only in the context of a world as circumscribed as Mrs. Jackson's. Although the *Biographical and Historical Memoirs* entry for the Jacksons states that Mrs. Jackson was an active member of the Christian Church, and the Christian virtues are certainly apparent in her concern for her neighbors, there is a refreshing absence here of the pietistic moralizing so common in other nineteenth-century rural diaries. The writer of this diary does not have an interesting mind, nor is the picture the reader gets of her particularly flattering; sympathy with her need to count every penny is tempered by the suspicion that her zeal at it signals a streak of meanness. But there is no doubt that she is telling the truth or that the life she depicts was shared by millions.

2. Francis Butler Simkins, *The South*, p. 254.

Desha County, one of the delta counties of southeastern Arkansas, has within its borders the confluence of the White and Arkansas rivers as well as that of the Arkansas and the Mississippi. In addition, it is crossed by bayous and creeks and is rich in lakes and swamps. This accident of geography has been both blessing and curse for the progress of civilization in the area, because continual flooding by these rivers and streams until 1928 built up deep layers of alluvial soil, making this not only some of the richest farmland in the world, but also extremely difficult to settle. The floods washed away roads, bridges, railroads, and even Napoleon, the county seat, between 1862 and 1874. It was this last event that gave Watson, in 1874, some hope for a future. The village nearest the center of the county and a station on the newly built section of the Little Rock, Pine Bluff, and New Orleans Railroad, Watson was the logical site for a new county seat. L. W. Watson donated five acres of land as well as material for a courthouse, and the county offices were moved there on 6 October 1874.[3] Henry Thane, in a memoir printed in *The McGehee Times* on 17 April 1930, described what Watson was like on the eve of this event.

> The day after my return from Collins I went up the other [rail]road to Watson, a distance of 28 miles. The road was on top of the levee, then only six feet high, to the mouth of Red Fork Bayou. The levee then turned westward to Amos Bayou. The road continued up Red Fork Bayou to the west, to Watson. . . . From there the bayou turned east to the Arkansas River and the road continued north to Medford, the next station. . . . Watson was all hustle and bustle. The county seat was being moved to it. Some half dozen buildings had been put up, including one for a saloon, and other buildings of different kinds.[4]

But the Watson boom was short-lived. Between 1871, when it became obvious that the county government would

3. *Biographical and Historical Memoirs of Southern Arkansas*, p. 1000.
4. Henry Thane, "Early Days in Southeast Arkansas," p. 30.

have to be moved from Napoleon, and 1874, when the move took place, the constant flooding of the tracks sent the railroad company into bankruptcy. It was reorganized as the Little Rock, Mississippi River and Texas Railroad, but the owners decided to construct a new line on higher ground, bypassing Watson completely.[5] When the new line was completed in 1879, the old one was abandoned and Watson lost its excuse for retaining the courthouse, for this circumstance strengthened the hand of influential people along the Mississippi and Arkansas rivers who had always wanted a river port for the county seat, as the waterways provided the most reliable means of transportation. Napoleon had been chosen in the first place because it was uniquely situated as port town for both rivers; when it washed away, there was no other port to replace it. Then, Arkansas City, a port on the Mississippi, was removed from Chicot County and annexed to Desha County, and it was decided in an election in September 1879 to move the county government there. This was done on 6 December 1880, and Watson was left without the county seat but with some of the functions of government, since it was decided to have duplicate courts in Watson as a convenience to residents in that part of the county who would have trouble getting to Arkansas City over the bad roads. Two circuit courts and four probate courts were held there annually until 1891.[6] This vestigial function as county seat was probably one of the few signs of life in Watson in 1890. Without it, the isolation would have been almost absolute. There was a dirt road north to Red Fork, the nearest port town on the Arkansas, where the town's supplies came in; another to Pea Ridge, a farming community six miles to the west; and another to Arkansas City, some twenty miles southeast. The road to Arkansas City was so bad that each leg of the trip required an over-

5. Mrs. L. A. Emerson, "History of Railroads in Arkansas and Desha County," p. 23.
6. *Biographical and Historical Memoirs*, p. 1000, and an unpublished history of Watson written by Jim Merritt of McGehee, p. 11.

night stay along the way. The difficulties of travel may be seen in an account written by Miss Fannie Owen in a letter to her good friend Miss Sallie Jones in June 1893 of a trip from Arkansas City to Tillar, a distance of less than twenty miles.

> We went from Arkansas City for about 2 mi. in a skiff then from there to 2 mi. beyond Trippe on a hand car, went through water 6 in. deep just pouring over the track then from there to McGehee in a wagon and from McGehee to Tillar on the train. Didn't we have a time getting there.[7]

Freight came to Red Fork on steamboats and was hauled to Watson in wagons. Mail came three times a week until 1890, when daily service was introduced. The only newspaper in the county was the *Arkansas City Journal*, a four-page weekly paper.

The land around Watson is absolutely flat, and in the 1890s the forest was all around. The following contemporary description by Octave Thanet is of northeastern Arkansas, but if the train is removed, the picture is probably a close approximation of Watson in 1890.

> Every traveler going south from St. Louis can recall the average Arkansas village in winter. Little strings of houses spread raggedly on both sides of the rails. A few wee shops that are likely to have a mock rectangle of façade stuck against a triangle of roof, in the manner of children's card houses, parade a draggled stock of haberdashery and groceries. To right or left a mill buzzes, its newness attested by the raw tints of the weather boarding. There is no horizon; there seldom is a horizon in Arkansas—it is cut off by the forest. . . . Generally there are a few lean cattle to stare in a dejected fashion at the train, and some fat, black swine to root among sodden grasses. Bales of cotton are piled on the railway platform, and serve as seats for half a dozen listless men in high boots and soft hats. Occasionally a woman, who has not had time to brush her hair, calls shrilly to some child who is trying to have pneumonia by sitting on the ground. No one seems to have anything to do, yet everyone looks tired, and the passenger in the Pullman wonders how people live in "such a hole."

7. Unpublished letter from Fannie Owen to Sallie V. Jones in the Jones Family Papers.

Two months later the "hole" will have changed into a garden. The great live oaks will wave a glossy foliage of richest green. Men will be ploughing in the fields and the negroes' song will float through the open car window. The house yards will be abloom with Japan quince and lilacs. The very shop windows will have a dash of fresh color in summer bonnets and poles of new prints. Then the stranger will waken to the charm of the South; and were one to leave the train and to stay in one of these unimpressive towns for a few weeks, he would come to appreciate that charm.[8]

This combination of dreariness and charm can be discerned in Mrs. Jackson's account of daily life in Watson, for the isolation contributed to the quality of life in both positive and negative ways. The limitations of being totally dependent on local resources for interests and entertainment are justifiably complained about by Mrs. Jackson. However, a positive aspect of that isolation can be seen in the powerful sense of responsibility for each other developed in the residents, who take on some of the aspects of a huge extended family. For example, one of the first entries in this diary notes that the cutworms have eaten up the family garden, the only source of vegetables; however, few days pass on which neighbors do not share the produce from their own gardens with the Jacksons. Another manifestation of this sense of community is the way everyone rallies round to care for the sick and the dead. And the incidence of sickness noted in this one year is appalling; this is swamp country, so malaria and typhoid fever are endemic. Mrs. Jackson records her own chills and fever as well as those of the other members of the community, and the powerful medicines taken so routinely sound almost as severe as disease. The epidemic which kills so many in the spring of 1891 sounds like typhoid, probably the result of Red Fork Bayou's annual overflow into the wells used for drinking water. Malaria, though not as frequently fatal as typhoid fever, was ever present and debilitating, and almost everyone had it at

8. Octave Thanet, "Town Life in Arkansas," p. 333.

7

one time or another. The African explorer Sir Henry Morton Stanley, who lived for a few months in 1861 at Cypress Bend about fifteen miles from Watson, considered the malaria he suffered in Arkansas far worse than the type he later contracted in Africa. His description of its effects corroborates Mrs. Jackson's descriptions of chills and fever suffered by various members of her family.

> It was a strange disease, preceded by a violent shaking, and a congealed feeling as though the blood was suddenly iced, during which I had to be half-smothered in blankets, and surrounded by hot-water bottles. After a couple of hours' shivering, a hot fit followed, accompanied by delirium, which about the twelfth hour, was relieved by exhausting perspiration. When, about six hours later I became cool and sane, my appetite was almost ravenous from quinine and emptiness. For three or four days afterwards, unless the fever was tertian, I went about my duties as before, when suddenly a fit of nausea would seize me, and again the violent malady overpowered me. Such was my experience of the agues of the Arkansas swamp-land; and during the few months I remained at Cypress Bend, I suffered from them three times a month.[9]

But Mrs. Jackson tells of other social gatherings in Watson than those in sickrooms and at wakes. People go to "dinings," "candy stews," school "speakings," and occasional dances, and they visit each other constantly. She also illuminates the amount and quality of communication between blacks and whites. This shadowy dimension of Southern culture has always been difficult to define, for segregation never meant that the races were kept separate; it simply meant that theoretically there were fairly rigidly prescribed paths for communication to take. Practically, however, there was a tremendous amount of flexibility, with immediate circumstances always providing the determining factor. Although there are no figures showing the ratio of blacks to whites in Watson in 1890, according to the census, of the 10,324 people in Desha County, 8,205 were black and 2,119

9. Henry M. Stanley, *Autobiography*, p. 156.

were white.[10] By consulting the census rolls for 1880 and 1900, it is possible to determine which of Mrs. Jackson's acquaintances were black and which were white. Readers unacquainted with the ways of the rural South of that time may be surprised to find how much communication there was between the races. Mrs. Jackson expresses friendly and affectionate feelings for a large number of blacks, and judging from their gifts and visits during her confinement, the affection was returned. She writes and receives letters for them, trades poultry and dairy products with them, does their sewing, and in the process of these transactions does a great deal of "visiting." The midwife who comes and stays for several days when the baby is threatening to arrive is black, and later, when that midwife and two friends move to Pine Bluff, Mrs. Jackson records how much she regrets seeing them go. Anyone uninformed about the race of the individuals mentioned in this entry would have a difficult time sorting them out:

> Wednesday, August 6, 1890. . . . I cut & made one of the aprons for Aunt Francis' grand child & Lizzie & I partly made the basque Aunt Chaney came & washed the dinner dishes. . . . Mrs. Chandler, Fannie, Mrs. Watson & Myrtle McEncrow were here a while this evening, Aunt Jane Osburn was here too, & Aunt Mary Williams she brought me a nice mess of squashes for dinner. Caroline Coalman is sick & sent Rosa to me to send her a piece of beef I sent her bucket full of cold vituals . . . got no letters to day wrote one for Aunt Francis to her mother & she took it to the post office, I gave her 50 cents for the 2 chickens she brought & a peck of meal for the dozen eggs . . . .

Aunt Mary Williams, Aunt Jane Osburn, Aunt Francis [sic] Hines, Caroline Coalman, Rosa, and Aunt Chaney are all black. The code regarding black-white relations dictated forms of address. Blacks could never be addressed as *Mr.* or *Mrs.*; those commanding respect because of age could be called *uncle* or *aunt*. All others were to be addressed by their

10. United States Census Office, *Bulletin*, no. 216, 1891.

9

names alone. This can be confusing in a document like this where there are also references to genuine aunts and uncles of the writer as well as to aunts and uncles of white friends who get the title from Mrs. Jackson as a matter of respect, like Aunt Minnerva Malpass. The only instance of overt, malicious racism in this diary comes when some young people put on blackface to be amusing. It is a mark of the time and place that even people as poor as the Jacksons had occasional black domestic help.

While evidence of this constant communication between whites and blacks does not imply any measure of social equality between them (it is impossible to imagine that Mrs. Jackson invited her black friends in to sit in her front room or to take a meal with her family), it is evidence of a type of mingling that would have permitted cultural influence to go both ways. For example, the highest praise Mrs. Jackson gives for a present of food goes to the yeast corn bread made and brought by one of the black women. This type of casual but seldom-recorded contact between blacks and whites was undoubtedly as integral a part of the fabric of Southern society in the nineteenth century as that other evidence of contact, the large number of mulattoes listed for Red Fork Township in the 1880 census.

As another mark of the time and place, the forms of address used by Mrs. Jackson for white men and women are worth noting, as they point to a far more formal code of manners at all levels of society than present custom requires. She always calls her husband, although he is ten years younger than she, "Mr. Jackson." This seems to be the rule for all white men over the age of, say, twenty-one, who are at her social level or above it. Day laborers like Will Emmit and others below her rank are referred to by their names alone. Women of any age who outrank her are "Miss" or "Mrs.," and sometimes those who do not, like Nellie Smithee, get this mark of respect. (Nellie Smithee may, in fact, have outranked her before Mr. Smithee's death.) Fannie Morgan is always simply "Fannie" until Miss Fannie Owen comes to stay, and then, probably to avoid confusion in the diary, she is called "Mrs. Morgan."

Most of the people mentioned in this diary were small farmers, in the same financial class as the Jacksons. A few, like the Nadys, were in the planter class, although for the most part the large plantations were closer to the river than Watson. There were also two or three doctors and several store clerks; some of the people mentioned held offices in the county government. The newness of the settlement is evident in the fact that few of the residents were born in Desha County, or even in Arkansas.

As for the principals in this journal, Nannie Stillwell Jackson was born 26 September 1854 in Fayette County, Tennessee, the daughter of Abraham and Tabitha Hudson.[11] It is impossible to determine where she grew up, but her close ties with people like the Edingtons, who are known to have left Napoleon, Arkansas, as it was sinking into the Mississippi River, suggest her own family's residence there. Nannie Hudson married Asher C. Stillwell, a merchant and farmer, on 16 December 1873. He died thirteen years later, on 10 August 1886. They had three children, William A., born in 1875, Etta Elizabeth, born in 1878, and Mary Sue, born in 1881.[12] William apparently died sometime between 26 June 1887, the date of his last extant letter to his mother, and 11 June 1890, the date of the first entry in this diary. Etta Elizabeth, or "Lizzie," married James Conner Coose and lived at Nady, across the river in Arkansas County, until her death in 1962. Mary Sue married John B. Graves and lived on the family place in Watson until her death in 1970.

When Nannie Hudson Stillwell married William T. Jackson on 1 August 1889, she was a thirty-five-year-old widow

11. *Biographical and Historical Memoirs*, p. 1026.
12. The *United States Census* for 1880 and 1900.

and mother of two young daughters and he was a twenty-five-year-old widower. Born in Jackson County, Tennessee, on 29 September 1864, William was brought to Arkansas at the age of nine when his widowed mother, Caroline Jackson, married John W. Cheatham and moved to Napoleon. The family later moved to Watson, where William was married on 15 September 1886 to Rachel Evans, who died in August 1887 after bearing a daughter who died in infancy.[13] William T. Jackson also survived Nannie Stillwell Jackson, who died in 1908, but the date of his death is unknown. According to the census, their children were Stonewall J., born in 1890, and Carrie M., born in 1895. The dates of their deaths are not known, but family tradition has it that they never reached adulthood.

The relationship between the Jacksons was complicated and difficult. Judging from her level of education and the social position of her first husband, it seems fair to say that it was a relative step down for Nannie Stillwell to marry this practically illiterate young man ten years her junior. The *Biographical and Historical Memoir of Southern Arkansas* notes that W. T. Jackson's "advantages were limited in his youth, and at the age of sixteen years he was compelled to begin the battle of life for himself, and first worked as a farm laborer, and tilling the soil has since been his occupation at which he is doing well."[14] According to Virginia Sue Meade, Mrs. Jackson's granddaughter, family tradition has it that W. T. Jackson drank heavily, which may explain why he declined to tell his wife where he was going "out in the town."

Asher C. Stillwell, on the other hand, came from a land-owning family of early settlers in Desha County and, judging from his letters, was as literate as his wife. Stillwell Point, named for his family, can still be found on the Arkansas River near Pendleton Bridge. He was appointed post-

13. *Biographical and Historical Memoirs*, p. 1026.
14. Ibid.

master at Watson in 1878, and the census for 1880 places the family somewhere in Red Fork Township, presumably in Watson. He assessed sixty acres of land in the vicinity of Watson in 1886, but surviving letters to his wife place her and the children at Selma, a community some thirty miles southwest of Watson, from December 1884 to February 1886, while Mr. Stillwell was living in Watson as a boarder in the home of Dr. Thomas Chandler and working in a store belonging to T. J. Lannon. When he died in 1886, he was buried in Selma. Perhaps Mrs. Jackson moved back to Watson at that time, for their son Willie Stillwell wrote his mother at Watson from Selma on 26 June 1887. Slipped between the pages of the diary is the following poignant bill from a merchant in Watson, made out on the back of a blank subscription order for the *Apostolic Guide*:

Mrs. Stillwell Dr. to J. M. Chiles	
To building one house	$30.00
" 575 boards	2.80
" 100 lathin	1.00
To making one coffin	5.00
	$38.00
	10.65
	28.15
	.45
	$28.60
Mrs. Stillwell cr by cash	
cash paid by self	5.00
To bill of goods	5.65
	$10.65

Although this bill is undated, the fact that it is addressed to Mrs. Stillwell in Watson suggests that it is the bill for making Mr. Stillwell's coffin and for constructing the house that the family occupied after his death, built on the land assessed by him in 1886 and transferred to her name on the Tax Record for 1890.

By references to the unpleasant changes that have come

13

in her life since the death of Mr. Stillwell and her insistence that she be buried next to him in the Selma graveyard rather than at Watson, Mrs. Jackson makes it plain that she does not like Mr. Jackson very much. Since their differences are made so obvious and not one glimmer of affection appears for him in this diary, one wonders why she married him. Any answer must be conjectural, but probably necessity, not romance, fostered this marriage. They needed each other for very practical reasons. On her side, there was no respectable way for a widow without substantial financial resources to support herself and two young daughters. The sixty-acre farm that Asher Stillwell left was not enough land to support them as rental property, nor could they make a living by farming it themselves. Her only skills were sewing and caring for boarders, neither pursuit lucrative enough to provide a living. A husband with a little property of his own and a willingness to work could make the difference between a decent standard of living and outright poverty. By the same token, W. T. Jackson needed her; in the course of this diary she helps him learn to write. The Desha County Tax Records for 1890 show that Mrs. Jackson assessed sixty acres of land and W. T. Jackson eighty acres. One-hundred-and-forty acres of good, cleared bottom land like this were enough for a decent living, but the Jacksons' financial problems suggest that some of this land must have been still in woods at this time; some of it was certainly underwater every spring. Mrs. Jackson's strong sense of "mine" and "his" in money matters may come from the fact that she entered this marriage with property of her own and the stewardship of what little Asher C. Stillwell left to provide for his children. Judging from evidence in the diary, Mr. Stillwell's estate was left in the hands of W. H. Burnett, a merchant at Pendleton, to be distributed in goods from the store and cash for the benefit of the Stillwell children. These resources were used up in the spring of 1891.

In spite of their age difference and the difficulties enumerated in this journal, the Jacksons make a life together. They share Sunday afternoon naps; he builds a pantry and shelves for her; she in turn tries to sew shirts that please him. When the baby is born, he even helps a bit with household chores. By the last entries, they seem to have reached a kind of accommodation with each other.

But if Mrs. Jackson's marital difficulties are spelled out, it is also made clear that it is the support of her women friends that sustains her. Men are on the periphery of the "real" life of Mrs. Jackson and her friends. Their situation is much like that described by Marilyn French almost a hundred years later in *The Women's Room*.

> There were two cultures—the world, which had men in it, and their own, which had only women and children. Within their own world they were there for each other physically and emotionally. They gave, through good humor and silent understanding, support and affection and legitimacy to each other and to the concerns they shared. Mira thought they were more important to each other than their husbands were to them. She wondered if she could have survived without them. She loved them.[15]

Nannie Jackson's support system consisted of some twenty women with whom she visited frequently, five she saw almost daily, and one she saw at least once and sometimes as many as four times a day. This was her best friend, Fannie Morgan, who lived the equivalent of about three city blocks away. At the beginning of the diary, Nannie Jackson was thirty-six years old and Fannie Morgan was the nineteen-year-old wife of a man seventeen years her senior.[16] She had recently lost a baby, which is possibly why Nannie Jackson was so solicitous toward her. They shared a great many things, including food, settings of eggs, flower cuttings, starch, household chores, and their troubles.

15. Marilyn French, *The Women's Room*, p. 113.
16. Since an Asher Morgan was listed in the census for 1880 in Asher C. Stillwell's household as his nephew, age two, there is obviously kinship between the Morgan and Stillwell families. However, so many family records have been lost it is impossible to determine what the kinship was. It may account for some of W. T. Jackson's suspicions of the relationship between his wife and Fannie Morgan.

Thursday, June 19, 1890. . . . I went up and washed the dishes for Fannie & helped her so as she could get an early start to washing for she had such a big washing Sue churned for her, Mrs. Nellie Smithee helped her wash & they got done by 2 oclock . . . I baked some chicken bread for Fannie & some for my self, & she gave me some dried apples & I baked 2 pies she gave me one & she took the other I made starch for her & me too, & starched my clothes & ironed the plain clothes & got dinner.

Although Mr. Jackson felt threatened by this friendship, the rewards of the relationship with Fannie were obviously more valuable to his wife than the rewards of sacrificing it for his sake would have been:

Friday, June 27th. 1890. . . . I did some patching for Fannie to day & took it to her she washed again yesterday & ironed up everything today I also took 2 boxes of moss & set out in a box for her, when I came back Mr. Jackson got mad at me for going there 3 times this evening said I went to talk about him . . . & said I was working for nothing but to get him & Mr. Morgan in a row, & to make trouble between them & I just talk to Fannie & tell her my troubles because it seems to help me to bear it better when she knows about it. I shall tell her whenever I feel like it.

And tell her she does. When she feels sick and depressed, for example, she asks Fannie to make sure that all of her possessions go to Lizzie and Sue and that she be buried next to Mr. Stillwell, her first husband, if she should die. The relationship with Fannie is as close as the tie between very close sisters, for she is as concerned about sickness in Fannie's household as in her own and seldom makes a special dish without taking part of it to Fannie. It is interesting that when the women in this network bring presents of food to each other they are not meant to be shared by the family at mealtime but are personal presents meant to be eaten on the spot. Although Mrs. Jackson does not mention it until the baby is "brought by Dr. and Mrs. Chandler" on 15 August 1890, she is pregnant when the diary begins.

Mrs. Jackson's other close friends are Mrs. Chandler,

Fannie Morgan's mother; Mrs. Nellie Smithee, a widow who works around the neighborhood as live-in domestic worker and field hand; and the Owen sisters, Miss Carrie and Miss Fannie, who have no home and board at the Jackson house during the term while Miss Carrie presides as the teacher of the one-room school. The Owen sisters are also like sisters to Nannie Jackson, but not as close as Fannie Morgan. The bond of wifehood is missing, that world of experience to which unmarried women are not privy. Nannie shares chores and food with Mrs. Chandler and Mrs. Smithee, but not, it appears, her troubles.

> Monday, June 23rd. 1890. . . . I made a berry pie for Fannie & sent it up there for dinner. I fixed both of Lizzie's new skirts & finished heming my new sheets, Mrs. Smithee came & brought me a cup of good pot licker & some greens & a piece of corn bread O but it was so good, & I did enjoy it so much. I let Mrs. Chandler have 7 pounds of meat to day, she is to pay it back Wednesday.
> Thursday, Feb. 12th 1891 Cloudy & drizly all day Cousin Mamie & Mr Jackson & Robert all got off early this morning & Sue & I milked & cleaned up & then I took Sue & the baby to Fannie's & she took care of them & Nellie & I went down to Mrs. Howells & got 2 sacks of greens, oh but they are nice we had lots of fun going down & coming back, she rod pomp & I rode Selim, I almost made Lizzie's drawers & begun my gown. Mr. Jackson got the house nearly done to day.

Miss Carrie, the only independent woman in this network, not only supports herself and presumably her sister, but also maintains her own horse, Denmark. Since the average pay for teachers in Desha County in 1890 was $252 per year, her independence was limited, but she is given the respect due her as an educated, self-supporting woman. While in the Jackson household she takes part in the social life of the community and joins in the sewing, but not the other household chores of the women. Mr. Jackson also resents her and complains because his wife will not reveal the subjects of their conversations to him.

The amount of visiting among the women in the larger

group is impressive because of the time and distance involved. This was not a community where houses were close together; separated by fields and pastures, they were at least a quarter of a mile away from each other. Moreover, the road was alternately dusty and muddy, and the bayou that runs through the area had to be crossed on a log. After heavy rains had swollen it the only way across was by boat. But the women managed to visit. In one sense, they had to, ᵢor in the absence of hospitals and funeral homes they were all responsible for each other. Everyone took turns "sitting up" with the sick and the dead. Men saw to making coffins and digging graves while the women were responsible for taking care of the household chores of the families involved and making pillows and face cloths for coffins. For example, on 2 August 1890, a little boy died in the Atkins home:

> August 2nd. 1890 . . . have done no work to day but house work, helped the children clean the yard & went to Fannies a while this morning, & she went down to Mrs. Atkins & took Lizzie with her & Mrs Chandler took Sue with her, they all came back by one oclock, I got dinner & then took a nap & then went with Fannie over to Mrs. Caulks & stayed a while . . . then home to get supper Lizzie churned & then went down to sit up at Mrs. Atkins, Fannie, Ella, Nellie, Alex Hazel & Brother Dick all gone down to set up.

But there is evidence in this diary of other kinds of social structures in Watson than the network of friendship among women. It is possible to see how the spheres of men and women differed, and the ways in which boys and girls were acculturated for their different roles. The following passage may show some of the differences between the activities of men and women:

> Friday Jan 9th 1891 . . . Mr. Jackson took a load of cotton to Redfork, & Brother Dick worked for Mr Dyer today & Will Emmitt did nothing but milk, cut wood & get a bout. Mr. Mayson Chiles went home so drunk this evening that he was unable to drive his team he fell out of his buggy once & Mr. Morgan drove it for him & Mr. Jackson went too they got him

18

home & put to bed then they came back & went to the candy pulling at the schoolhouse.

Most of the activities that took men out of the orbit of the immediate neighborhood were not open to women; men had to go out in the world to do their work; women had to stay near home to do theirs. Travel was arduous because of the bad roads. Even when women worked in the fields, as those on the Jacksons' economic level had to, the character of the work was different from that done by the men because it was impossible for women to aspire to the running of a farm as their life's work. Women were considered to be more or less occasional field hands who did the most menial labor, like hoeing and picking cotton, while men and boys not only hoed and picked, but planted, plowed, and hauled the product to market. People who do only menial tasks are not considered as responsible as those who drive teams, and they do not make decisions nor acquire the other skills necessary for running a farm. Moreover, a farmer had to know how to do everything connected with farming, from well digging to carpentry, skills passed down from men to boys, while girls were locked in the women's culture, learning only the housekeeping skills that are passed down from women to girls. Using a hoe and putting cotton in a sack is unskilled labor at its lowest level, never leading to anything better for people who are not permitted the hope of rising to a position of managing and making decisions.

It is easy to see how little girls in this community were acculturated to follow in their mothers' footsteps. Lizzie and Sue worked right along with their mother at household tasks and spent their free time playing dolls and mimicking the roles of adult women.

Sunday, June 15th, 1890. Cloudy & warm sun shine a little, brisk south wind all day, Mr. Jackson went down to Mr. Howells this morning did not stay very long, he came back ate a lunch then went up on the ridge & helped Mr. Morgan to drive home Lilly & Redhead the 2 cows that I am to have the milk of, Lilly is mine but Redhead is not she is in Mr. Morgans care

19

& he lets me milk her, I sent Lizzie up to help Fannie clean up this morning & I baked 2 green apple pies & took one to her she sent me some clabber for Mr. Jackson's dinner, Lizzie & Sue did not want to go anywhere to day & they stayed at home all day & played with their dolls & had sunday school & a doll dinner out under the plum tree, I slept some read some & wrote sister Bettie a long letter . . . . Lizzie Sue & I have spent a pleasant day.

Predictably, Lizzie and Sue married owners of small farms and lived much the way their mother had. Lizzie moved some thirty miles away across the Arkansas River to the next county, and Sue settled down with her husband on her mother's property in Watson and remained there until her death in 1970.

Although over the past ninety years Watson has passed through more prosperous times, especially when the surrounding forest was being cut for lumber and while it was the center for the maintenance crews for the Missouri Pacific Railroad, which eventually ran a successful line from New Orleans to Memphis through Watson, its public aspects today do not appear to be very different from what they were in 1890. There is a post office, a branch of the McGehee bank, a couple of service stations, four churches, a liquor store, two grocery stores, and 431 inhabitants. The trains no longer stop in Watson, and the depot has been torn down; the road through town was graveled about 1930 and then paved with asphalt about 1954. The school has classes through the fourth grade; the other students are bused to a consolidated county school ten miles away. Most of the woods that surrounded the town have been cut, and the flood control system of levees instituted after the 1927 flood has allowed the potential of the rich farmland to be realized. Farms tend to be larger now, and soybeans and rice are as important cash crops as cotton. The Jackson house is gone and so are the public buildings that were there in 1890, except for possibly one or two large brick buildings on the main street. They are abandoned.

However, the point cannot be overstressed that Mrs. Jackson's diary bears witness to more than the heritage of this moribund community in the Delta. The isolation and dullness of life there, the very tedium that is the stuff of this record, are the heritage of the entire rural South as well as of large areas of the rest of the country. For example, there are many points of similarity between the quality of life portrayed here and that depicted by Henry Conklin in his 1891 memoir of his poverty-stricken boyhood on one hard-acre farm after another in upstate New York. Both documents are testimony to the back-breaking labor, the boredom, the incessant struggle to survive, and the limited prospects of marginal farmers. But there is an interesting and instructive difference between the attitude of the people in Watson and that of Conklin's people, who believe that just over the hill, or the next county line, or further west they will find the perfect farm where their lives will become infinitely more satisfying. The Jacksons and their friends are not on the move; they do not seem to expect to improve their lot by picking up and going somewhere else. Perhaps it was the richness of the soil that kept them from dreaming that grass elsewhere might be greener. After all, Henry Conklin's Uncle Joe dreamed of a farm "that did not have a stone on it big enough to kill a chipping bird," where the oats would grow as tall as a man.[17] It is a sobering thought that the Jacksons owned such a farm, and the living they got from it was the realization of the American rural dream.

17. Henry Conklin, *Through Poverty's Vale*, p. 76.

THE DIARY

[June 1890]

Wednesday, June 11th. 1890. Clear some cloudy some & warm, Sue[1] & I hoed some this morning & Lizzie[2] & Sue this evening Mr. Jackson[3] & Lee Hickson finished planting the corn to day & Mr. Jackson hoed & Lee broke the millet ground this evening, Fannie's[4] hen I set for her died on the nest to day & one of my hens quit her nest, I sent the eggs to Fannie & she put them under a hen up at her house & I let out a hen I had put in the coop to break from setting & she took the eggs the banty had quit Lizzie & Sue are at home to night, Ed Gordan[5] ate his supper at Fannies to night he was here for dinner we have not seen him any more to day Lula Gifford[6] [several lines are illegible]

Thursday, June 12th. 1890, Cloudy some, clear some, the children hoed all day & did very well I hoed some in the yard about along my flowers, Fannie & I hoed some in the garden the cut worms are so bad we have not got scarce any thing left in there I got a long letter from sister Bettie Miller,[7] to day, Ed Gordan is still sick & laying about at Miss Fannie's. Nellie[8] talks of leaving Mrs. Dyer[9] & wants to hoe for

1. Mary Sue Stillwell (1881–1970) was the daughter of Nannie Stillwell Jackson and Asher C. Stillwell. She married John B. Graves and lived on the Stillwell place in Watson until her death.
2. Etta Elizabeth Stillwell (1878–1962) also was the daughter of Nannie Stillwell Jackson and Asher C. Stillwell. She married James Conner Coose and lived at Nady, Arkansas, until her death.
3. William T. Jackson was born in Tennessee in 1864 and came to Arkansas at the age of nine when his mother married John W. Cheatham. He and Nannie Hudson Stillwell were married 1 August 1889.
4. Fannie Morgan, born in 1871 in Kentucky, married Charles B. Morgan, a farmer at Watson, in 1887. Charles B. Morgan was born in 1854 in Arkansas. Fannie was the daughter of Dr. and Mrs. Thomas Charles Chandler. The Morgans were the Jacksons' closest neighbors.
5. Ed Gordan was a local handyman and farm laborer.
6. Lula Gifford was born in 1878 at Watson, the daughter of Charles and Annie Gifford.
7. Bettie Miller cannot be identified with certainty, but she appears to be Mrs. Jackson's sister.
8. Nellie Smithee made her living by doing domestic and field work in the neighborhood. She seems to be a widow.
9. This is probably Mrs. E. R. Dyer.

25

Mr. Jackson but we have not got any place for her to stay Mr. Jackson turned Ed off to day & told him to go about some until he got able to work but I dont think he will go any where,

Friday, June 13th, 1890 Clear some cloudy some very warm, I washed this morning & got done by 5 minutes after ten then read a while & cooked dinner did it all by myself as Lizzie hoed all day & did a very good days work Mr. Jackson [line illegible] I went over to Mrs. Giffords[10] & stayed about an hour, Josie[11] is sick but not very bad, Fannie sent me a saucer of butter it was enough for dinner & supper we did all enjoy it so much. I feel very well tonight. Ed Gordan ate dinner here he still stays at Fannie's Mr Jackson turned him off Wednesday but he has not went anywhere yet, Fannie sent me a nice bowl of hominy for our dinner it was so nice, have been too busy to write to sister Bettie today.

Saturday, June 14th, 1890. Clear some cloudy some one lite shower of rain did not last very long, I put out a bed but had to take it in on account of the rain, Mr Jackson borrowed a mule from Dr. Chandler[12] & worked it all day, he plowed me up more rows in the yard to plant some garden seed, I got a quarter's worth of seed & planted them & some mustard. I hope I can have a few things to eat after a while, I sent Lizzie to Mrs. Dyer's & got some green apples to make me some pies, I bought me 12 yds sheeting, 12 yds of domestic 6 spools thread & had all that charged but I got a pair of stockings for Lizzie & paid for them, they were too small & I sent Lizzie back & she got a larger pair, & I kept the others for Sue, she paid for the ones she got, I got

10. Annie Gifford was born in 1843 in Tennessee. She was the widow of Charles Gifford, a grocer and farmer at Watson, and mother of Charles H., F. John W., Josie, and Lula Gifford.

11. Josie Gifford was born at Watson in 1876. She married Cam McNiel.

12. Dr. Thomas Charles Chandler was born in Illinois and moved to Watson from Memphis. His children were Fannie (Morgan), Ella, James, and Earl J. Chandler.

no letters today, I ironed when I got dinner & parched a pan of coffee for Fannie & she almost made Lizzie a bleach domestic skirt. I finished the skirt & hemed one sheet, I made 5 sheets out of the 12 yds, & I let Fannie have one to get her to make some triming for Ella Chandler that Lizzie started to make but she has not got time to make it, & to let me have a dozen eggs to set a hen, l went up to Fannie's this morning & helped her clean up the house & then she went to the store with me, the children got done chopping cotton by 4 o clock now all the cotton has been choped over once & [illegible] once, Lee finished breaking the ground for millet today he plowed Beppo & Mary & he left before sundown. [illegible] was not here for supper, Fannie ate dinner here she made me a vinegar pie & it was so good, she gave me some fresh butter milk for my dinner, it looked like Mr Jackson got mad because I bought what I did today but I can't help it if he did.

Sunday, June 15th, 1890. Cloudy & warm sun shine a little, brisk south wind all day, Mr. Jackson went down to Mr. Howells[13] this morning did not stay very long, he came back ate a lunch then went up on the ridge & helped Mr. Morgan to drive home Lilly & Redhead the 2 cows that I am to have the milk of, Lilly is mine but Redhead is not she is in Mr Morgans care & he lets me milk her, I sent Lizzie up to help Fannie clean up this morning & I baked 2 green apple pies & took one to her she sent me some clabber for Mr. Jacksons dinner, Lizzie & Sue did not want to go any where to day & they stayed at home all day & played with their dolls & had sunday school & a doll dinner out under the plum tree, I slept some read some & wrote sister Bettie a long letter fixed up 7 journals to send her, & cut a piece out of a paper that Mr. Jackson brought from Little Rock to send her, he has not stayed about the house but very little today, Lizzie Sue & I have spent a pleasant day. Ella Chandler came

13. James S. Howell was born in 1825 in Tennessee. His wife was Martha and their children who are named in this diary are Iola, Iona, and Charles J.

& stayed a few minutes out with the children she did not come in the house, there is a heavy cloud & thunder & I think we will have rain before midnight, it rained a heavy shower before sundown. Nellie Smithee was here for a few minutes late this evening, Mr. Jackson asked where was the postpaid envelopes he bought & why I did not use them & I said he bought them & I did not propose to use them & he did not like it & he gave them to Lizzie & to Sue.

Monday, June 16th 1890, Clear & warm, I let Lizzie go help Fannie this morning & Sue & I washed, Fannie gave me some butter & milk for my dinner, Mr. Jackson milked Redhead and got about a half galon of milk, we got done washing before ten oclock & saved the suds & Lizzie & Sue scoured the kitchen, Mr. Jackson hoed some for Henry Reed this morning & fixed a gate at Pete's,[14] & this evening he went in the woods & got a load of planks & then up in town & got a block & sill & at half past 3 oclock he begun the store room & got it almost half done, Lizzie Sue & I set out some more flowers, the ones that Fannie had in boxes on a shelf on her galery & I fixed a bucket of moss & gave her, did a little mending this evening, set one hen got a dozen eggs from Fannie, she has been here twice today. I let her have a ten lb bucket of flour this evening, Lizzie has been suffering all day with something like the flux, she is better tonight, the children did not hoe any to day because it was too wet, Mr. Burnett[15] came down this evening.

Tuesday June 17th 1890. Clear & very warm until about 3 oclock then it rained a rite hard shower, the children hoed all the morning & about a half an hour after dinner, Mr. Jackson almost finished the pantry today he hoed some & plowed some & then when the rain put an end to the field

14. Peter Willis was born in 1854 in Georgia. He was black.
15. William H. Burnett, Jr., was born in 1857 in Arkansas. He was a planter and merchant with a store at Pendleton, a community some ten miles from Watson. When Asher Stillwell died, the assets left to his children were left in W. H. Burnett's hands, there being no bank in Desha County at the time.

work he & the children moved the corn, I packed boards for Mr. Jackson to cover the pantry with & then changed my dress & went over to see Mrs. Chandler & stayed nearly 2 hours, & this evening I did some mending, I got no letters today. Lizzie got one from Mrs. Jane Mask,[16] Fannie stayed with her ma all day today. Harry & Willie[17] stayed here, Harry hoed some for Mr. Jackson to day, Mrs. Chandler had another bad spell last night like she had last summer she is better today. Fannie & Nellie stayed with her last night & are to stay there again to night, Lizzie went up & churned for Fannie this evening & ate supper there & then went over to Mrs. Chandler's with Fannie & then came home & took her bath & went to bed, I wrote a few lines more in my letter to sister Bettie & sent it & the papers off today,

Wednesday June 18th, 1890. Clear & warm oh so warm I put some of the things out of my kitchen into my pantry & turned my table & safe around & now I have so much more room, Sue washed a lot of my jars & I set them in the pantry on the shelves Mr. Jackson made for me yesterday, I went to see Mrs. Chandler again today she is better was setting up some, then Fannie & I went by Mrs. Dyers & got some greens & plums, Fannie got the greens to put with some she had & when she cooked them she gave me some & some pot licer. I had a nice saucer of greens at Mrs. Chandlers this morning she sent me some potlicker yesterday evening, Mr. Jackson went to Dr. Chandlers this morning & got 3 doses of calomel for Lizzie & I gave it to her, she is better to night. I wrote Cousin Lizzie Burnett[18] a letter to day &

16. Jane Mask was born in Alabama. The census for 1880 lists her as housekeeper in the house of John R. Chiles. A letter written from her to Nannie Jackson in 1906 places her in Jennings, Missouri.

17. Harry Morgan was born in 1881. Willie Morgan was born after the 1880 census and apparently died before the 1900 census. They were Charles B. Morgan's sons by his first wife.

18. Elizabeth Coose Burnett was born in Tennessee and married W. H. Burnett. She is the mother of W. H. Burnett, Jr.

sent by Mr. Jackson, he & Mr. Morgan went to Redfork this morning, they started before eight & now it is after 9 & they have not got back, I made 2 new hen nests to day & white washed 2 old ones & burned the straw that was in them & took off another hen with ten little chickens. Mr. Burnett left yesterday evening & did not fix up the books again, Mr. Morgan was down here a while today he says I must not let Lizzie hoe very long at a time, I made 4 plain pillow cases for Fannie this evening; & had to rip the hems & hem them the second time for I did not do it rite at first. I hemed one sheet for my self & started another, Fannie made Lizzie a nice domestic skirt today & gave it to her, she put embroidery on it it is made with a deep ruffle, now Lizzie has 2 she is alrite, I am tired & sleepy & I do wish they would come on, Asher[19] went with his Pa & Harry with Mr. Jackson.

Thursday, June 19, 1890. Clear & warm, very warm Lizzie is a heap better today. I went up and washed the dishes for Fannie & helped her so as she could get an early start to washing for she had such a big washing Sue churned for her, Mrs. Nellie Smithee helped her wash & they got done by 2 oclock, Mr. Morgan & Mr. Jackson went back to the landing this morning & got the freight, it was after ten oclock last night when they got home the boat was so late & the roads so bad they did not try to bring the freight. Asher & Harry had to stay at Cousin Lizzie's alnight, Mr Morgan ate dinner here & then helped Mr. Jackson to unload the freight then Mr. J. went up & helped him unload his, Mrs. Cheatam[20] was here a few minutes at dinner time she came to see Dr. Chandler about her eye somthing bit or sting her over her right eye monday night & her face is

19. Asher Morgan, born in 1878, is Charles B. Morgan's son by his first wife. The census for 1880 lists him as the nephew of Asher Stillwell, in whose home he is residing. The relationship between the Stillwell and Morgan families is unclear.

20. Caroline Cheatham [sic] was born in 1846 in Tennessee. She was W. T. Jackson's mother.

sweled rite bad & she cant see out of that eye, Mr. Jackson had to take Mary to the Allen place[21] again today when he came back by his ma's she sent me a pint can full of butter it is nice & enough of it for 2 or 3 meals I churned to day for the first time, Lizzie & I hoed some in the yard to day. Mrs. Gifford, Josie, & May all came to see me this evening I did some mending to day. Mr. Jackson got him self a pound of tobacco this morning. I baked some chicken bread for Fannie & some for my self, & she gave me some dried apples & I baked 2 pies she gave me one & she took the other I made starch for her & me too, & starched my clothes & ironed the plain clothes & got dinner. Lizzie got a letter from her Cousin Mamie Caldwell[22] & she sent her brother Ashers picture he is a fine looking lad of 19 summers, I got no mail at al,

Friday, June 20th, 1890. Clear & very warm Lizzie washed some to day I helped her a little. Mr. Jackson plowed all day to day, I hoed some in the yard again this evening, the children washed their heads to day it has been so hot I have not done very much sewing to day, Mrs. Nellie Smithee went to Mrs. Chandlers this evening to make it her home for a while, Mrs. Chandler was here a while this morning so was Fannie she brought home the soap she owed me & also some artificial flowers for Lizzie's hat. Lizzie seems alrite to night. Lizzie churned for me again late this evening & I made some butter more than I made yesterday, Mr. Jackson got mad at me about the hoes. I did not under stand him & I could not get him to understand me & he quarreled agoodeal at me about it rite at the supper table,

Saturday, June 21st, 1890. Clear & warm so warm went to Mrs. Dyers soon this morning & got some plums & apples

21. The Allen family cannot be identified. Mr. Jackson seems to be taking the mare there to be bred.

22. Mamie Caldwell was the daughter of Nannie's sister Mollie, who lived in Campbell, Kentucky.

got some for Fannie too, made some apple pies, & ironed my starched clothes & got dinner, Mr. Jackson got Wash to work for him to day & he got his millet planted & harrowed off, & he plowed in the cotton the rest of the day until late this evening & then he plowed the irish potatoes. Ed Gordan hoed them thursday, I got no letters to day. I paid Mrs. Chandler the big dishpan of flour I owed her. Mr. Jackson carried it to her, Mrs. Hall is at Fannies to night she came to see me this evening & stayed a little while, Mr. Jackson, fixed a place in the pantry & put the meat in there & he also nailed up a box in there for me & Lizzie pasted paper all in it & on the out side too, I have got pretty well fixed in my pantry & I do like it so much, Mr. Jackson got him self a pair of shoes & a pair of socks this evening, he also fixed a frame for the cypress vines[23] this evening, I am tired & sleepy to night he did not get home until after ten o clock & set up & waited for him, he took his bath then went to bed to sleep he did not stay awake to talk but *little*,

Sunday, June 22nd, 1890. Clear & warm oh so warm some south breeze, Mr. Jackson put Mary on the grass in the field & I thought he was going to stay at home with me but he did not he went somewhere else then came at 11 o clock got Mary & sadled her ate a lunch put on another shirt & left to be gone about [illegible] hours he said but it is nearly sundown & he has just come, I have read some & slept a heap & wrote a long letter to Mrs. Gates in Selma,[24] 6 pages, large letter paper, & Lizzie wrote Mrs. Jane Mask 2 pages fools cap & Sue wrote to her too. Fannie came this evening & brought me a bowl of blackberries & oh they were so nice I just ate all I wanted gave the children some. Lizzie Hall came & stayed a while with the children this evening & played & behaved very well,

23. The cypress vine is a flowering vine in the morning glory family.
24. Mrs. Gates cannot be identified. Selma, Arkansas, is a community about thirty miles southwest of Watson where the Stillwells were living before his death and her final move back to Watson.

Monday, June 23rd. 1890. Clear & warm until after [illegible] o clock then it clouded up we had a shower of rain. The children hoed some this morning & Lizzie helped her Cousin Fannie to wash some Willie Morgan is quite sick. I have been up there twice to day they are giving him calomel Aunt Frances Hines[25] was here a while to day I wrote a letter to Anna for her, I made a berry pie for Fannie & sent it up there for dinner. I fixed both of Lizzies new skirts & finished heming my new sheets, Mrs. Smithee came & brought me a cup of good pot licker & some greens & a piece of corn bread O but it was so good, & I did enjoy it so much. I let Mrs. Chandler have 7 pounds of meat to day, she is to pay it back Wednesday. Mr. Jackson did not go out in town after supper to night he stayed at home with me, I sent the coffee to Pete Willis in return for the tea Mr. Jackson got last thursday.

Tuesday, June 24th. 1890. Clear & very warm, Lizzie washed to day did not get done until nearly 3 o clock I helped her rinse & hang out, & Fannie helped her some too. I hoed some in the cotton late this evening Sue helped me, I have been up to Fannie's twice to day Willie is not much better, Aunt Susan Watson was here a while this morning & I gave her a pitcher of milk. I also gave Pete Willis some milk to day Asher helped Mr. Jackson plow corn to day. Mr. J. hitched Jim the young horse up single & plowed him single about half the evening, I got no mail today but an Ark City Journal.[26] I lent Mrs. Chandler the quilting frames to day & she sent Nellie & Ella after them, I have got another hen hatching. I wrote a letter to Alice Reddick for Charlie Hicks today & sent it off,

25. Mary Frances Hines was born in 1833 in Virginia. She was black.
26. The *Arkansas City Journal*, edited in 1890 by D. A. Gates, was published as a Democratic newspaper. *The Biographical and Historical Memoirs of Southern Arkansas* characterizes it as "a four-page seven-column sheet, ably edited and well printed, the only paper now published in the county, and regarded as one of the best local papers in the state."

Wednesday, June 25th. 1890. Clear & warm all evening cloudy & foggy in the morning Lizzie & I hoed 15 rows of cotton by 9 o clock, then we came in took a bath & changed our dresses & I took a nap then went up to Fannies. Willie is not very much better, after I got dinner I went up to Fannie's & helped her patch some & brought some home to do for her, for she has got so much to do, Asher helped Mr. Jackson plant corn all day to day, Mr. Jackson took sick in the field about sundown & is rite sick to night, Mr. Morgan came down & stayed a while to night & he sent some pills by Asher, he went back & asked his ma for some snuff for Mr. Jackson, Lizzie carried water this evening & let Sue rest & sleep, Mr. Jackson was to have hired Mike Goodman to work for him but he went down the bayou to day & I dont know why he would not work for us. I saw Maggie Stroud[27] today [illegible line]

Thursday June 26, 1890. Clear & warm until after 4 o clock then we had a big rain, Asher hoed for Mr. Jackson today & Lizzie & Sue hoed some too, Mr. Jackson was sick all day & could not work he tried to hoe some but did not do very much, I did not cook any dinner to day. I gave Aunt Susan Watson some more sour milk today & a little sweet milk too done a very little patch[ing] to day slept some & read some. Fannie was here a little while this morning, Mr. Jackson is better to night, I got no letters to day, Ella Chandler came here for some more meat this evening, Lizzie caught & killed & picked the little duck leged rooster for to cook for Mr. Jacksons breakfast in the morning it is one of the little chickens that I kept all through the overflow there are 3 left now, one rooster & 2 pullets.

Friday, June 27th. 1890. Clear & warm, clouded up late this evening but it did not rain any here. Lizzie washed today & was until 3 o clock getting done she washed her doll clothes

27. Maggie Stroud was born in 1862 in Arkansas. She was the wife of Hadley Stroud, a farmer and merchant at Red Fork.

& I made starch & she & Sue starched their doll clothes. Sue washed her doll clothes tuesday, I did some patching for Fannie to day & took it to her she washed again yesterday & ironed up everything today I also took 2 boxes of moss & set out in a box for her, when I came back Mr. Jackson got mad at me for going there 3 times this evening said I went to talk about him, he got mad & said I was working for nothing but to get him & Mr. Morgan in a row, & to make trouble between them & I just talk to Fannie & tell her my troubles because it seems to help me to bear it better when she knows about it. I shall tell her whenever I feel like it he accused me of mean things because I was going to send to Redfork by Mr. Morgan to get some white goods to make Sue & I a white dress apiece oh but I would rather he had treated me with silent contempt for 6 months than to talk to me as he did this evening & when he saw how it hurt me & made me cry then he wanted me to kiss him & make up, I kissed him but I can never get over what he said, he is going to keep on quarreling at me until he makes Lizzie leave home for good. Mr. Jackson took Mary down to the Allen place again to day he did not get back until 3 o clock he borrowed Sam from Mr. Morgan, & when he came home Sam got sick & Mr. Jackson had to drench him. Asher hoed this evening for Mr. Jackson. Pete Willis sent me some fish & I sent him some milk. I sent 3 of the fish to Fannie after I fried them. Tony sent me a bucket of blackberries & I did enjoy them so much, I sent Fannie a saucer full of them,

Saturday. June 28th. 1890. Clear & warm, Lizzie & Sue ironed & I parched coffee & got dinner, they did not get down their doll clothes we swept the house good & turned Lizzie's & Sues bed around & they scoured the galery, I did some mending & took a nap & hoed some in the yard, the only hen I had setting quit her nest today & I gave the eggs to Fannie she was gone berry picking & I took them up there & put them under two hens she had setting, Mr. Jackson drove the little wagon & Fannie Nellie & Ella went &

got some berries, the children stayed here with me; Ed Gordan worked some for Mr. Jackson today so did Asher, I got no mail today but some papers, Fannie was here a little while late this evening. I did enjoy the berries so much have cooked what we did not eat & am to make a pie to morrow, John cut some stove wood for us this evening. Mr. Jackson tried to get Ed Gordan to cut it but he would not. Mr. J. also paid Asher for the work he done for him this week a dollar & a quarter.

Sunday, June 29th. 1890. Clear & very warm clouded up late in the evening & a lite shower of rain, Sue & Lizzie have been at home all day Sue wrote to Mrs. Chiles[28] & Lizzie to her Cousin Mamie Caldwell, I have read some & slept some have been home all day, Mr. Jackson lent Beppo & the little wagon to Mrs. Hall & she went home today she got a mule from Dr. Chandler. Ed Gordan drove the wagon & went & Asher went too I sent Mrs. Sallie Watkin's[29] basket home it has been here 3 weeks yesterday, Fannie went up to see Mrs. Winters to day, Mrs Hall sent Mrs. Chandler some irish potatoes & Fannie some cabbage Fannie sent me some of the cabbage & she sent me some green apples this morning & I am going to make me some pies to morrow if nothing happens to prevent me. Mr. Jackson stayed out tolerable late last night he has not been going out in town after supper any hardly this week, Ed Gordan was here yesterday for breakfast dinner & supper & here for dinner to day. Mr. Jackson & I took a nap late this evening & before I got up Mrs. Chandler came & called me & I walked down to the school house with her, came back & woke Mr. Jackson up & we ate our supper & then went up to the lot & caught Winn, my leghorn rooster & put him in the hen-

28. Mrs. Chiles cannot be identified with certainty. The Chiles family was prominent in Watson.

29. Sallie A. Watkins was born in 1868 in Arkansas and was married to William T. Watkins, of Red Fork. She is the sister of Miss Fannie Owen and Miss Carrie, the teacher who boards with Mrs. Jackson.

house, then went up to Fannies & while we was there Brother Jim[30] came, he brought me a letter from Miss Alfie Edington[31] & 2 nice heads of cabbage that Mrs. Brown on the ridge[32] sent me.

Monday. June 30th. 1890. Cloudy, warm & threatened rain all the morning but brite & hot all the evening, Lizzie washed to day & got done by 3 oclock, Aunt Minnerva Malpass[33] & Cousin Lizzie Burnett came down to day, Aunt Minnerva came to see me before dinner & Cousin Lizzic after dinner, they ate dinner at Fannies, I have not done any work scarcely to day cut out some pillow caces this evening Lizzie churned to night so she would not have it to do in the morning Mr. Jackson went out in town after supper but he did not stay very long Brother Jim gave Fannie & the children some lead pencils & they gave us all 2 a piece which made 8, I am so glad to get them for I was needing a pencil so bad Lizzie went to the store & got her 20 cts worth of blue calico & I have cut & partly made her bonnet.

[July 1890]

Tuesday. July 1st. 1890 Clear & warm until late in the evening then it clouded up & looked like we was going to have a storm but it did not last very long & no rain I sent Lizzie up to Fannies to help her wash but she did not wash to day so Lizzie helped her clean up. Fannie has been at Mrs. Dyers most all day, Mrs. D is cutting & fitting her white dress & is going to make it, she & Fannie was here a while just after dinner. Mr. Jackson got 5 yds of domestic

30. Brother Jim seems to be Mrs. Jackson's brother.
31. Alfie Edington was the daughter of Jilson Edington. Formerly of Napoleon, the Edington family lived at Pea Ridge in 1890.
32. Mrs. Brown cannot be identified, but the "ridge" is Pea Ridge, a community six miles north of Watson.
33. Minnerva Malpass was born in 1832 in Tennessee. She was married to Franklin Malpass.

& I cut & made him a shirt to sleep in. Lizzie did the most of the machine work. I have not felt well today am afraid I am going to be sick I went up to Fannies a little while late this evening & was talking to her, & I told her to see after Lizzie & Sue if I was to die & not to let me be buried here have me taken to Selma & put beside Mr. Stillwell[34] & I want Lizzie & Sue to have *every thing that is mine*, for no one has as good a rite to what I have as they have I have been married to Mr. Jackson just 11 months to day & it seems like a heap longer time, maybe if we had got a long better the time would not seem so long. A daily mail has been established[35] & Brother Jim came out to carry it on this end of the rout but the contracter failed to let him have it & he went back to Dumas to day & is to come back to night & stay here the balance of this week, he took Nellie Smithee out a buggy ride yesterday evening, Mr. Jackson plowed yesterday & to day so did Ed Gordan, he & Walter (Petes boy) planted the corn to day. Ed has been here to eat regular yesterday & to day, I got no letters today just some papers,

Wednesday, July 2nd. 1890. Cloudy some clear some & hot oh so hot, I have felt tolerable well to day, have patched some & finished Lizzies bonnet all but the splits, Fannie washed today & Lizzie helped her & they all came here for dinner & Brother Jim too it is the first time he ever has eat here since Mr. Jackson & I have been married, I got no mail today, Mr. Jackson hoed in the cotton to day & Ed Gordan plowed Mr. Jackson went out in town to night & has not come yet he did not stay out very late last night, Nellie Smithee was here a little while this evening Mrs Stroud was

34. Asher C. Stillwell was born in 1846 in Arkansas and died 10 August 1886. He was appointed postmaster at Watson in 1878. His last extant letter, dated 30 March 1886, shows him boarding at Dr. Chandler's in Watson while Nannie and the children are living in Selma.

35. According to the *Post Route Map of the State of Arkansas and the Indian Territories*, mail was delivered to Watson and Red Fork three times a week in 1884. Presumably, July 1890 marks the first daily delivery Watson has had.

here a little while yesterday evening, I made starch & starched Mr. Jackson's shirt & then sent the other to Fannie & she starched her clothes,

Thursday, July 3rd. 1890. Clear & pleasant quite warm all morning but a nice breeze all evening. Lizzie & I washed & got done before elevin o clock & I ironed the starched clothes & got dinner too & then went to Fannies & got a new piece of jeans to patch Mr. Jacksons pants he hoed again all day today & Ed plowed in the cotton Sue carried water all the morning & Lizzie all the evening Fannie & Harry ate dinner with us I cooked my duckleged rooster for dinner had him stewed with dumplings I also made a bread pudding. they all seemed to enjoy their dinner I patched some then went over to see Mrs. Dyer & stayed about an hour, Pete Willis hoed for Mr. Jackson this evening. Sue was a little sick this evening but she seems alrite to night, John Hornbuckle[36] is carrying the mail, I got none to day,

Friday, July 4th. 1890, Clear & warm, Lizzie carried water all the morning and Sue all the evening, Mr. Jackson hoed some & plowed some & so did Ed Gordan they finished the lower cut of cotton I got no letters to day just 2 papers, I patched Mr. Jacksons pants & Sues dress & darned his socks & Lizzie washed some to day, Fannie ironed Ella helped her, I went up there a little while this evening & she gave me just as much onion as I could eat, & I did enjoy it so much she gave me some fish & I cooked it for supper & stewed the head & we all enjoyed it, Brother Dick[37] came this evening he is going to work a month for Mr. Jackson he gave Lizzie & Sue a dime apiece this is the second time I ever saw the 4th of July pass & it did not rain

36. John Hornbuckle, born in Watson in 1869, was the son of Martha Hornbuckle.
37. Brother Dick is Mr. Jackson's brother Richard Jackson, born in Tennessee.

Saturday, July 5th. 1890. Clear & warm & windy I made some plum jelly for Fannie & cooked me some apples & made 2 pies & made one glass of apple jelly for myself, Brother Dick was here for breakfast dinner & supper so was Ed Gordan Ed hoed some in the corn this morning, I trimed Sues hat to day Mr. Jackson sent to Redfork by Mr. Morgan & he got Sue a dress with the money Brother Jim & Brother Dick gave her I got no letters today Mr. Jackson took Mary down to the Allen place again to day, I went up to Fannies & then over to Mrs. Chandlers a while this evening Mr. Jackson went fishing this evening & got a nice mess for supper he has not worked any to day Sue is sick to night I had to give her pills, Lizzie ironed for me to day

Sunday, July 6th. 1890, Clear & warm Lizzie went to church with Mr. Morgan they went horse back, she rode Mary, Fannie went in the buggy with her ma & they took Willie with them, Brother Jim took Mrs. Smithee in his cart & they came here & ate their dinner when they came back from church. Ella rode Sam & went with Alex Hazel Mr. Jackson lent Beppo to Ed Gordan & he rode her & went he was here for breakfast & dinner Mr. Jackson stayed at home most all day, Brother Dick has been sick all day he has a high fever to night he got some medicine from Dr. Peoples,[38] I wrote to Alfie Edington wrote her a long letter, Lizzie wrote to Lizzie Edington, we are going to send them by Brother Jim when he goes out to Dumas, Mr. Jackson & I went up to Fannies & stayed a little while to night after supper she is sick taking pills,

Monday, July 7th. 1890. Clear & very warm Lizzie packed water from the bayou to wash with. I went up to Fannies & stayed a while she is better, Mr. Will Watkins[39] & Miss Sallie came & stayed all the morning with us I do think their baby

38. S. J. Peoples was born in 1841 in Tennessee. The census for 1880 lists his occupations as doctor and farmer.
39. William T. Watkins was born in 1866 in Arkansas.

is so pretty they ate dinner with us they went over to see Mrs. Chandler & Mrs McNiel.[40] & after they left Lizzie & I washed all the clothes & put them out I let Sue go home with Miss Sallie, oh but I was so glad to see her come this morning & I hope she will come again, Ed Gordan ate breakfast here he has gone to work for Doc Chandler, Brother Dick is not much better, I am tired & sleepy Mr. Jackson plowed in his corn to day, he got me 50 cts worth of writing & 20 cts worth of stamps to night, he did not stay in town long to night,

Tuesday, July 8th. 1890. Clear & very warm until late in the evening then it turned cooler but no rain, Mr. Jackson plowed in his corn again today, I did not do very much work to day, went up to Fannies & she & I went over to see Mrs. Caulks[41] baby it is sick, Mrs. Simmons is staying at Mrs. Caulks but she did not come where we were, I borrowed the tucker from Fannie Blanch White[42] brought me an undershirt to make for her I cut it out but did not do very much on it, got no mail today, Mr. Stroud gave me a paper to sign that Judge Pindall[43] left at the store for me I have to take it to Mr. Alfie McNiel[44] to sign. Brother Dick is better to night, I feel tired & sleepy Nellie helped Fannie wash to day, Lizzie has had to carry water in Sue's place & she could not help her Mr. Morgan ate dinner here to day, he brought me some apples from the place this evening, Asher took pills to day he is not sick much,

40. Mary McNiel was born in 1844 in Virginia. She was married to Alfie McNiel and was the mother of Cam McNiel.
41. Mattie Gifford Caulk was half-sister to Josie and Lula Gifford and was the wife of Benjamin Caulk.
42. Blanche White was born in 1864 in Arkansas. She is listed in the census for 1900 as a head of household, farmer, and black.
43. Judge Xenophon J. Pindall was born in West Virginia in 1835. He settled in Napoleon in 1866 and practiced law there until the county seat was moved to Watson, where he practiced until 1878, when he was elected circuit judge and moved to Arkansas City. He was the uncle of Xenophon O. Pindall, acting governor of Arkansas from 15 May 1907 to 11 January 1909.
44. Alfie McNiel, born in 1841 in Mississippi, was a dry-goods merchant and farmer.

Wednesday, July 9th. 1890. Clear & hot oh so hot up to about 3 o clock then it clouded up & we had a rite nice little shower but not near enough, I most made Blanch's under shirt today, & cut her a chimise, I also made 4 lemon pies for dinner got 6 eggs from Aunt Mary Williams.[45] I cooked my apples too after the rain Mr. Jackson & I went up to Mr. McNiels & I signed the rite of way to the railroad company,[46] Brother Dick hoed some today so did Mr. Jackson I made starch & starched my clothes to day & had some left & took it to Fannie & starched what she had & she gave me a bucket of clabber & I made some curd, I sent my letter to Miss Alfie to day by Brother Jim he went home to day, he took Nellie out for a ride yesterday evening & then after they came back he took Ella, Ella & Mrs. May stroud went to see Mrs. Hunleys baby Frank,[47] he is very sick. & Fannie & Mrs. Stroud went to day & stayed half the day, I feel very well to night, I got no mail to day Brother Dick bought the lemons for the pies Mr. McNiel looks fearful bad he has been very sick Mr. Morgan ate dinner here to day, Fannie Smith & her little sister Polly came here & stayed a while this morning I dont know what they came for, I put my bed out to sun & had to take it in by 3 oclock, on account of the rain

Thursday, July, 10th. 1890. Clear & hot not enough rain yet, I finished Blanche's skirt & almost made her chimise Mr. Jackson plowed in his corn & Brother Dick hoed in the cotton, I have not been to Fannies today she came here a little while this evening, I gave her some fish Mr. Jackson bought 30 cts worth of cat fish today, no mail for any of us

45. Mary Williams was born in 1814 in Kentucky. She was black.

46. This must have been the right of way for the line finally laid through Watson in 1904 by the North Memphis, Helena, and Louisiana Railroad.

47. Betty Hundley [*sic*] does not appear in any contemporary records and seems to have died in 1891. Her sons, Edgar and Frank Hundley, are listed as boarders in the Hadley Stroud home in Red Fork in the census for 1900. Frank Hundley, who married Hattie Irby, was a merchant in Watson for some forty years before his death in 1959.

to day, I feel very well to night, Mr. Jackson got me ten cents worth of nutmeg & some spice too to night he did not stay out in town very late to night came home & went to bed before I got ready, Lizzie & I fixed to wash tomorrow,

Friday, July 11th. 1890. Clear & hot all day some breeze but still it was hot Lizzie & I washed & got dinner & scoured the kitchen & she churned & had to milk Lillie, this is twice this week she has milked her, I got the rest of the eggs from Aunt Mary to day & paid her for them, Blanch came & got her things & seemed pleased with them she is to pay me tomorrow Fannie has been here a little while & I have been there, Willie is sick again Mr. Jackson & Brother Dick plowed in the corn to day Lizzie carried water & came very near getting too hot. I feel very well to day.

Saturday. July 12th. 1890. Clear & hot, no rain yet & we do need rain so bad Mr. Jackson & Brother Dick did not do any work to day, Brother Dick stayed out in town most all day & Mr. Jackson went to Redfork in the morning & did nothing in the evening, he took his plows to the shop & got me a lawn dress. I made it mother hubbard and Fannie has one like it we made them today she helped me & I helped her the lawn only cost 5 cents a yard she got another dress but it is different it has 12 yds in it & she is going to make it tight waist & full skirt. Mr. Jackson got them for us, he also got 12 yds of goods to make him three shirts he brought some onions & irish potatoes & I got dinner in a hurry oh but I did enjoy the onions so much, Lon Howell came up this evening & stayed a long time with Lizzie, she is over at Ella Chandler's to night. Ella was here twice to day she made Lizzie a doll hat, Lizzie went over there & stayed 2 hours, Mrs. Chandler was here a little while this evening I went up to Fannie's & basted while she sewed & we got both the hubbards done, Mr. Morgan Asher, Harry, Emit & Ed, all went fishing & got a nice lot I did not eat any, Mr. Jackson ate some up at Fannie's, I did not want any, Lizzie & I ironed this morning & got done by ten oclock, Sue is at Miss Sallies yet, when ever she comes home I am going to let Lizzie go & stay a while, I got no mail to day there has been a daily mail for nearly 2 weeks & I have not got a letter yet, Blanch White paid me the 75 cts she owed me, I gave Mr. Jackson a nickle to get me some Pearline, there was none there but he spent the nickle all the same.

Sunday, July 13, 1890. Cloudy some clear some & very warm; some breeze from the south but no rain yet, Brother Dick is sick again today he could not eat any breakfast, Fannie came down this morning & we went out & got a mess of raddishes for her & I, & I boiled the tops & had a very good mess. Ella Chandler came again to day she & Mrs. Smithee & Lon Howell were all here for dinner, I happened to have plenty cooked & we all ate & enjoyed it if it was a cold dinner, Mrs Smith & her 3 children came here this morning & stayed about an hour & a half, I gave one of her little girls Lizzies hat that she had out grown, Mrs. Chandler & Mrs Howell went to Mrs Winns today, Mr. Jackson went out in town & stayed until after ten o clock last night & night before last too we are all well to night Brother Dick went up to see his ma this evening he rode Mary my horse, Mr. Jackson lent Jim to Bufford to ride to day to see if he can get him broke when Brother Dick brought me a pound of nice butter when he came home. Mr. Jackson & I went up to Fannies & stayed a little while.

Monday, July 14th. 1890. Clear some cloudy some & a little rain late this evening, still very warm Lizzie & I washed & got dinner & got all done by 2 oclock, then I took a nap & did a little mending went up to Fannies a while this morning, Mrs. Chandler was here a little while, I wrote a letter to the doctor at Dumas for her, Fannie came down a while this evening she made her other lawn dress today her ma helped her, Mr. Jackson plowed his corn this morning &

Bro. Dick took Mary to the Allen place this evening they both worked on the cypress logs to make pickets Ed Gordan came & got his clothes to night I guess I am done washing & mending for him, I got 2 papers & a printed letter from the Goodspeed Publishing Co, in Chicago, Ill. Mr. Jackson did not go out in town tonight all at home & all well Mrs. Nellie Smithee made Lizzie's doll a hat today.

Tuesday. July 15th. 1890. Cloudy & rainy some but not enough rain yet still very warm, cut Mr. Jackson 3 shirts & made one except stitching the collar & the buttons & button holes, Miss Fannie Owen[48] & Mr. Will Watkins came to day brought Sue home & took Lizzie back with them Miss Sallie & the baby are well as usual, Mr. Jackson & Brother Dick worked at the picket timber all day, today Mr. Will & Miss Fannie ate dinner here got no mail to day Fannie & her ma went to Redfork to day, Mr. Jackson went out soon after he ate his supper & it is nearly 9 oclock & he has not come back yet I had early supper last night & again to night, ate before we had to lite the lamp,

Wednesday July 16th 1890. Clear some cloudy & very warm but no rain yet, Mr. Jackson & Brother Dick finished working what timber they had sawed I went up to Fannies & stayed a while this morning & brought home her white dress skirt & riped the band & fixed it for her, & then got dinner & tried to take a nap & then finished the skirt & patched an old one & did some other jobs got supper, & wrote a letter to Mrs. Wilson in Ocalla, Fla, telling her we wanted one of Iola Howells pictures, lent Fannie the 75 cents that Blanch paid me saturday, she wanted to pay Mrs. Dyer for making her dress, Brother Jim came out from Dumas to day he was down here a while this evening, got no mail to day, Mr. Jackson is out late tonight, Livingston, our

48. Fannie Owen is the sister of Sallie Watkins and Miss Carrie, the teacher. See entry for Monday, 22 September 1890.

dog died this evening. Sue is going to bury her, she dug some in the grave this evening

Thursday, July 17th. 1890. Clear some cloudy some & very warm a *little* rain not enough to do very much good, Sue & I washed & got done & got dinner by elevin o clock Mr. Jackson & Bro Dick worked on the road to day, I made Mr. Jackson another shirt to day went up to Fannie's once but she was not at home & I did not stay long, I got no mail to day, Sue went over to Mrs. Giffords & stayed a while this evening, & Fannie came & brought the things & I put them away, Sue went to bury her dog this morning & Brother Dick burried it for her, he also brought me a barrel of water to wash with got it from the bayou. Cousin Dennie Stillwell came to day he is staying at Mr. McNiels, he & Katie went down to Mrs Howells this evening, Brother Jim went back to dumas to day

Friday, July 18th. 1890. Clear some cloudy some a very lite shower late this evening still very warm, I made the other shirt today now they are all done I went to Fannies & stayed a while this evening, Brother Dick & Mr. Jackson worked on the road again today, Mr. Will Watkins brought Lizzie home this evening as he would have a heap of riding to do next week & could not bring her, I cooked dinner & sent to Mr. Jackson & Brother Dick by Asher Morgan he rode Mary & took it, Fannie was here today a little while & I was there twice she ironed some this evening & so did I & after supper Mr. Jackson & I went over to Mrs. Giffords & set till bed time & it rained some & I borrowed a shawl & a pair of shoes for I wore old slippers & it was most too damp to come back with them on & Mr. Jackson borrowed a coat from Mr. Gifford, & it was so dark we fell over the end of a log & I got my nice clean white apron all muddy & tore the belt in two when I fell, I skined my left leg but dont feel hurt any other way, no mail today. heard that Mr.

Burnett & Miss Ruth McDaniel[49] are married & came home on the boat wednesday, Cousin Dennie Stillwell went out on the creek fishing to day with Kate, Adie & Cam McNiel[50] he has not been around to see us yet, to day is Brother Jims birthday he is 27 years old, to day a year ago I gave him a nice cake but this year I have nothing to make a cake of,

Saturday, July 19th. 1890. Clear & hot oh so hot, I made lemon pies & got dinner & then cut out Sues new dress & made it & did some mending, did not take time to sleep any to day, Miss Josie Gifford came & stayed a while this evening, Brother Dick went up to Mr. Morris he rode Beppo, Cousin Dennie came to see us this evening & ate supper with us & we had a real pleasant chat, Fannie brought me some fish & Pete Willis sent me some nice ones too, I got no mail but papers, Mr. Jackson Brother Dick & Walter Totten[51] worked the corn until dinner.

Sunday. July 20th. 1890. Clear & warm, clouded up some in the north but no rain yet & every thing is so dry, Cousin Dennie came & told us good bye & he has gone out in the back country. Cam McNiel piloted him across the creek, Fannie was here a while this morning she & Ella went down to Mrs. Chiles, Ella & Nellie Smithee & Mr[s.] Chandler were all here to day, & Mrs. Dyer came & stayed a while too, Mrs Stamp[52] came & spent the day with Mrs. Dyer & I went over there to see her she is teribly afflicted with boils, Mr. & Mrs. Caulk & Mrs. Simmons were all there Mrs. Caulks baby has got well & is a very pretty baby, Fannie,

49. W. H. Burnett's first wife, the former Sally McDaniel of Moulton, Alabama, died 12 April 1889. In July 1890 he married her sister, Ruth McDaniel.

50. These are the children of Alfie and Mary McNiel. Kate is twelve, Adie fourteen, and Cam twenty.

51. Although the Tottens are mentioned several times in this diary, they do not appear in any contemporary records and so cannot be identified. Three members of the family died of what seems to be typhoid fever during 1890 and 1891.

52. Elizabeth Stamp was born in 1846 in England.

Ella, Nellie, Elie Hazel, Asher, Harry Willie & Lizzie all went riding & they all had a horse a piece except Willie & he rode Pomp the mule, Oh my but they all had a gay time, Lizzie got scared of Mary the horse she was on & had to swap with Nellie & Willie complained that he could not keep up & Harry could not keep his saddle blankets, Brother Dick came back & brought us some roasting ears, some tomatoes & some irish potatoes oh but they are all nice we are all well, Mr. Jackson stayed all day with me I read some to him before we went to Mrs. Dyers & some after we came back, he went over to Dr. Chandlers with Brother Dick after supper but he did not stay long he has been so good & kind this last two weeks has not fussed about anything I have done like he used to, he got a little vexed about one of the shirts because I did not exactly understand him but I tried to fix it to suit him & I believe I did manage to please him after a while, I have about caught up with my work at last & I am so glad for may be I can get about some oh but it is tiresome to have to stay at home all the time. I have not been any where only where I could walk since I came home from Mrs Coopwoods[53] the first day of may, oh yes I went to see Cousin Bettie Sain twice in June when she was so sick, went both times at night, well I must be patient for my time will come after a while, then I can go,

Monday, July 21st. 1890. Clear & not quite so warm but still dry very dry, Mr. Jackson plowed in his corn & Brother Dick & Walter Totten hoed Lizzie & I washed & got dinner & she scoured the kitchen we got it all done before 3 o clock & I took my nap while Lizzie scoured, Sue carried water nearly all day, Lizzie carried some while Sue took a nap, got no mail to day, Mr. Jackson went out in town but did not stay long, Fannie & Harry went down to take Mr. Morgan & the hands their dinner they went in the cart & drove grey Nellie, Fannie went on & spent a while with Mrs. Howell,

53. Mrs. Coopwood was the wife of Benjamin J. Coopwood, a farmer near Pea Ridge.

48

Asher had a chill to day but he is not sick much, Fannie came down & set a while after supper, & Mr. Jackson went home with her, I did not do any sewing to day,

Tuesday, July 22nd. 1890. Clear some cloudy some but no rain yet dry & hot, some breeze all day Lizzie helped Fannie wash & they got done by 4 o clock, Lizzie & Sue are both complaining of feeling badly & I feel bad my self to night, I did some mending made 4 lemon pies got dinner & cut a dress & a basque for Aunt Mary Williams I got the waist stitched up & fit & the basque fit I got a letter from Miss Alfie this evening Fannie came down a while & I gave her some lemon pie, Aunt Mary brought me a dozen eggs that is to help pay for her dress Mr. Jackson got some more tobacco last night he went to the Allen place again today to take Mary, that was all he done this morning & this evening he cut millet for Mr. Alfred Stroud,[54] he took the childrens bottles over in town to sell for them after supper it is after 9 oclock & he has not come yet, he got himself a new knife to day, got a letter for Aunt Frances Hines[55]

Wednesday. July 23rd. 1890. Clear some cloudy some but no rain yet still very warm, made Aunt Mary's dress & basque all but the buttons & buttonholes made starch & starched the clothes & did some mending, got no mail to-day, Lizzie & Sue planted some raddishes this evening, Lizzie bought the seed with ten cents of her money she got for her bottles Sue paid Lizzie the dime she borrowed to help buy the green ribbon to put on her hat, Fannie came down a little while this evening, I have not been there yesterday nor today for I have been so very busy, I do feel so bad to night Mr. Jackson plowed in the corn nearly all day &

54. Alfred Stroud was born in 1855 in Arkansas. He was a successful merchant and farmer who is described in the *Biographical and Historical Memoirs of Southern Arkansas* as being "fond of fine horses and of hunting deer. This latter sport occupies him not a little, deer being plentiful in this portion of the country." He was married at this time to W. T. Jackson's stepsister, the former Lizzie Cheatham.

55. Mary Frances Hines was born in 1833 in Virginia. She was black.

Brother Dick hoed in the corn all day Walter Totten hoed all the morning but got sick this evening

Thursday & Friday July 24 & 25th. 1890. The 24 was windy & warm & dry. I finished Aunt Marys dress & basque & she brought me the eggs to pay for it 2 dozen more, Mrs. Howell came to see me for a little while Nellie came after she left & brought the baby. Fannie came twice once in the evening & then after supper, I had a chill & was very sick but Sue & I managed to get all the ironing done Aunt Francine Branch[56] was here a while this evening & she ironed some for me Lizzie was in bed all day I gave her pills today Mr. Jackson plowed in the cotton & Brother Dick hoed in the corn,

the 25th was clear & warm until about 2 oclock & then we had a lite shower & about four o clock a real *hard* rain oh but it did us all so much good, Lizzie & I washed & got done soon Mr. Jackson went to Red Fork yesterday & got me a quarters worth of Pearline & 25 cts worth of onions, & also bought a large bell & it was brought home today & he & Brother Dick & Alex Hazel put it up after the rain, I made 6 pillow cases to day went up to Fannies & stayed a while & she was down here a while after supper, Mr. Jackson sent the slippers he got for me, to Redfork by Doc & had them changed for a smaller pair & I like them very much. Mr. Jackson got a bottle of quinine & ten cents worth of salts for me I had to take some I have another chill this evening got no mail yesterday nor today, He got another bottle of medicine from Doc it cost a dollar, Mrs. Chandler was here a little while yesterday evening,

Saturday, July 26th. 1890. Clear & pleasant, patched some cut & partly made my new bonnet went up to Fannies a while. Mr. Jackson & Brother Dick did no work to day because it was too wet, Brother Dick went up to Mr. Coop-

56. Francine Branch did domestic work in the neighborhood. She was black.

woods & got a sack of potatoe vines & Mr. Morgan sent some where & got some too & this evening the whole crew got out & set out vines until after dark, Lizzie & Sue got supper, they both got a letter from Mrs Jane Mask, I got no letters only some papers, I sent the book & book satchel to Mrs. Coopwood by Brother Dick,

Sunday. July 27th. 1890 Clear & tolerably pleasant stayed at home all day until late in the evening & Mr. Jackson & I went up to see Mrs. Hornbuckle[57] & stayed a while, Fannie & Nellie came a while this evening & Brother Charlie[58] was here for dinner Lizzie & Sue fixed the most of the dinner John Hornbuckle was here a while to day, Lizzie wrote to Mrs. Carrie Embree today Aunt Chaney[59] & Emeline were here a while to night they brought me a loaf of light corn bread it is so good, Mr. Jackson & I had a good nap to day,

Monday July 28th, 1890 Clear & warm, Lizzie & I washed to day & got done by half past 9. then I rested a while & got dinner took a nap & then finished my bonnet, & went up to Fannies & stayed a while & wrote a letter to Miss Alfie Edington 8 pages of note paper, Fannie & Aunt Chaney was here a while, Aunt Chaney ate dinner here & I gave her some meal to make me some more, risen corn bread, Nick Osburn[60] died this morning, Mr. Jackson got some rice to night, he & Brother Dick plowed all day to day,

Tuesday, July 29th. 1890 Clear & warm we got up soon & I cleaned the house & dishes. & sue helped me & Lizzie cut a path from here to the pump, I fixed new cuffs on one of

57. Martha Hornbuckle, a widow, was born in 1833 in Tennessee. She was the mother of Laura, Sam, Louisa, and John Hornbuckle.

58. Charles Jackson, W. T. Jackson's brother, was born in Tennessee.

59. Aunt Chaney was the midwife who was expected to deliver Mrs. Jackson's baby. She was probably Chaney Turner, born in 1808 in Virginia, and the mother-in-law of Anna Binson, who is mentioned in the entry for 8 August 1890. Chaney Turner was black.

60. Nick Osbin [sic], according to the census for 1880, was born in 1842 in Arkansas. He was black.

his shirts & did some mending & fixed the skirt to Fannie's white dress again baked some molasses cakes ate an awful big dinner & have been so sick all the evening, Mr. Jackson & Brother Dick plowed all the morning & this evening Brother Dick went & got stuff & made 2 mauls & Mr. Jackson made us a wash shed & worked some on the fense Nellie Smithee is at Fannies again today she helped Fannie to wash today Lizzie bought a package of plain envelopes & paid for them, this morning,

Wednesday, July. 30th. 1890 Clear & warm until about 3 o clock then a big rain & pleasanter after that, went up & helped Fannie cut 4 pair pants & then showed her how to fix them came home & got dinner took a nap, Bell Howard & Ione Howell came & stayed a while here & then went up to Fannies & on over to Mrs. Chandlers, I went up to Fannies & got 2 pair of the pants & worked the button holes, I also did some mending for my self to day, Mr. Jackson went to Red Fork this evening got back after sundown he & Mr. Morgan went to gether, Mr. Jackson got a peck of onions & a peck of potatoes, I went up to Fannies after supper & stayed until he went to the store & back Brother Dick took Mary to the Allen place this morning he did not do any work this evening got no mail to day,

Thursday, July 31st. 1890 Clear some cloudy some no rain here, Lizzie washed to day got done by elevin oclock I helped her to rench & hang them up, after dinner I took a nap & then went up to Fannie's & stayed a while & then over to Mrs. Chandlers & set a while have not done any work today, but house work, Mr. Jackson & Bro. Dick have been diging a well to day Henry Reed helped this evening, Mr. Morgan is sick but not much Mr. Brown came out today from Dumas he said the folks were all well, I dont feel very well to night, Fannie & Nellie were here a little while this evening, Aunt Francine tried to make the soap for us but made a failure I got a bucket of the lie it will do to wash dishes, we had to pay her 50 cents for what she done, got no mail to day Mr. Jackson got a gallon of vinegar tonight

[August 1890]

Friday, August 1st. 1890. Clear some cloudy some & a very lite shower of rain, Mr. Jackson, Bro. Dick, & Henry Reed got the well done by twelve oclock & Mr. Jackson & Brother Dick finished putting in the curb & putting a shed over it this evening I been up to Fannies once today she has took medicine today & dont feel well Mr. Morgan is better Lizzie & Sue have gone up to Fannie's to stay all night for Alec & Nellie have gone to set up with Mr. Atkin's little boy who died this evening, I feel very bad to night, Aunt Chaney was here a while this evening, I did some mending to day & Lizzie washed Mr. Jacksons clothes he had on in the well, he & I got a letter from Mrs. Wilson this evening & Lizzie sent her letter to Miss Carrie[61] this morning Brother Dick has gone to sit up too down at Mr. Atkins. Lizzie got Aunt Chaney 5 cents worth of smoking tobacco this evening she paid for it her self, & gave it to Aunt Chaney, Cousin Van[62] cut Mr. Morgans hay to day, Mr. Jackson helped me clean the dishes to night

Saturday, August 2nd. 1890 Clear some cloudy some one lite shower still very warm, have done no work to day but house work, helped the children clean the yard & went to Fannies a while this morning, & she went down to Mrs. Atkins & took Lizzie with her & Mrs. Chandler took Sue with her, they all came back by one oclock, I got dinner & then took a nap & then went with Fannie over to Mrs. Caulks & stayed a while, then we went to Mrs. Dyer's & then to see Mrs. Chandler a while then home to get supper

---

61. Miss Carrie was the teacher who was soon to come to board.
62. Van R. Ryan was born in Arkansas in 1843.

Lizzie churned & then went down to sit up at Mrs. Atkins, Fannie, Ella, Nellie, Alex Hazel & Brother Dick all gone down to set up Mr. Jackson went down with Mr. Morgan to help him get in his hay & when he came back & found me gone he got mad, Bell Young was here a while to day she sent Fannie & I some apples this evening, I have a headache to night Mr. Jackson did not leave me last night after supper nor to night got no mail to day but a paper Mr. Jackson got a letter from Mrs. Sallie Wilson yesterday

Sunday, August 3rd. 1890 Clear & warm some breeze from the south, went up to Fannies & stayed a while this morning, Fannie & Ella went in the cart Mrs. Chandler took Harry Willie & Sue in the buggy with her, Nellie rode Sam, Alex Dixie, & Asher his pony bill, & they all went to the burying Mr. Jackson & Mr. Morgan went up early & dug the grave, I have had a nap & read some to day, Lizzie up in the wagon with the corpse, Brother Dick went to Redfork, when he came back he brought some lemons, Mrs. Chandler sent me a shoulder of fresh pork, I cooked it for supper, we are all at home & all well, Judge Pindall brought me a letter & a bundle of papers from Miss Alfie, lent Mrs. Chandler my water table out of the kitchen she sent Ed Gordan after it, wrote to Mrs. Wilson to night for Mr. Jackson, Josie Gifford was here a few minutes to day

Monday, August 4, 1890. Clear & warm, Mr. Jackson killed whiteface my tiny cows yearling & sold it for beef, he got the money for most of it, sent his ma a piece gave Mr. Morgan 15 lbs & sent Aunt Lucinda Black a piece, Lizzie Sue & I cleaned the tripe & feet, we did not get to eat breakfast until after six oclock & Mr. Jackson did not get all the beef sold until most sundown, I have felt so bad all day & dont feel any better to night got no mail to day but the Ark. City journal, Mr. Jackson has done no work today except to clean & sell the beef, Brother Dick hauled pickets to put around the fense, I made some more lemon pies today, we did not get to wash today because Fannie & Mrs. Smithee washed & then we had enough to do anyway. Lizzie & Sue went to see Myrtle McEncro she is over to Mrs. Giffords with Mrs. Watson they came yesterday & Mrs. Lawson came to day, Court opened this morning,[63] Mr. Jackson gave me ($5.25.) five dollars & twenty-five cents of the beef money & I have put it away to keep until I need it which wont be very long I dont reckon,

Tuesday, August 5th. 1890. Clear some cloudy some & a little rain, Lizzie was sick all day & Sue & I begun the washing & Aunt Frances Hines came & finished it for us, & she washed the dinner dishes Mrs. Cheatam & Katie was here a little while this evening Lizzie feels better to night & so do I. I made 4 lemon pies in pie pans & one deep pie in little press pan, borrowed 3 pans from Fannie & sent her a pie by Brother Dick, bought 2 chickens & a dozen eggs from Aunt Francis & cut a basque for one of her girls have done no sewing to day Fannie & Mrs. Smithee were here a little while this morning, got no mail to day, Mr. Jackson gave me $4,25 more & now I have nine dollars and a half in all & I am going to keep it for my own benefit when I get sick

Wednesday, August 6, 1890 Clear some & cloudy some I got Mr. Jackson to put my bed out but had to take it in on account of a shower of rain & I got sick too, I cut & made one of the aprons for Aunt Francis' grand child & Lizzie & I partly made the basque Aunt Chaney came & washed the dinner dishes & stayed all the evening & is here to night, Sue went home with Lon Howell & Lizzie is up at Fannie's. Mrs. Chandler, Fannie, Mrs. Watson & Myrtle McEncrow were here a while this evening, Aunt Jane Osburn[64] was here too, & Aunt Mary Williams she brought me a nice mess of

63. Although the county seat was in Arkansas City, court was also held in Watson for the convenience of people in the northern part of the county. Arkansas City was about twenty miles away over a dirt road.

64. Jane Osbin [sic], according to the census for 1880, was born in 1828 in Kentucky. She was married to Nick Osbin.

squashes for dinner. Caroline Coalman[65] is sick & sent Rosa to me to send her a piece of beef I sent her bucket full of cold vituals, I have been so sick nearly all day Lizzie & I managed to get the ironing done we are having a rite good shower to night, Brother Dick started work on the fense but could get no help & had to quit, Mr. Jackson has done no work to day he did not leave me much today & tonight, got no letters to day wrote one for Aunt Francis to her mother & she took it to the post office, I gave her 50 cents for the 2 chickens she brought & a peck of meal for the dozen eggs, Fannie gave Lizzie some pills to night, Mr. Jackson killed & almost sold out another beef this evening

Thursday, August 7th. 1890 Clear some cloudy some & threatened rain a heap but no rain yet, Aunt Chaney is here yet I have felt better to day, Mrs. Howell & Maggie Stroud came to see me today so did Mrs. Watson & Mrs. Thomas used to be Mollie Gifford, Tom Gifford came with her, they did not stay long, Mrs. Stamp spent the day in Watson to day she called by here twice she brought the books home & I gave her her book Stanleys' travels[66] & also Beadles travels[67] to read, Brother Dick took Mary to the Allen place again today & came by his ma's & she gave him some butter there is a dance at Dr. Chandlers tonight & Mr. Jackson & Brother Dick went, every one from Fannies went & Lizzie had to come home I feel bad yet, Lizzie & Aunt Chaney made their bed in the kitchen & slept on the floor, I sent Sue some more clothes by Mrs. Howell & asked her to keep sue until sunday, Mr. Jackson & Brother Dick did no work to day court broke today, Mrs. Chandler sent me a nice plate of

65. Caroline Coalman is listed in the census for 1880 as the mother of Frances Hines and Prince Coalman. She was born in 1833 in North Carolina. She was black.

66. This is probably a reference to Henry M. Stanley, *How I Found Livingstone: True Adventures and Discoveries in Central Africa* (New York, 1872). Note that the Jackson family dog was named Livingston.

67. This may be a reference to Charles Beadle, *A Trip to the United States* (London, 1887).

eatibles by Ed Gordan this morning & a nice dish of greens by Asher this evening oh but I did enjoy it all,

Friday, August 8. 1890 Clear some cloudy some & still very warm Mr. Jackson came home from the party at 3 o clock this morning & we all slept late, Aunt Chaney washed to day & got done before one oclock, Mrs. Chandler came to see me this morning & stayed a good while, Anna Benson[68] came to see us to day so did Aunt Emeline Davis, Mrs. Gifford came & stayed a long time she ate dinner with us, Mr. Jackson went to Redfork & was gone most all day Brother Dick slept about half the day I have been rite ailing all day but I feel better to night this makes 2 days that I have done no work, Lizzie got a letter from Miss Carrie this evening I got a paper that is all Mr. Jackson got Lizzie a dress to day at Redfork, very pretty calico just like one Ed Gorden got for Fannie, sent Lizzie to the widow Smiths & got me a nice mess of greens,

Saturday, August 9. 1890. Clear some cloudy some but no rain yet & very warm, cut & made Lizzies dress & then took her oldest cotton checked dress & made me a cook apron, made starch & starched 4 shirts for Mr. Jackson & one for Bro. Dick, Lizzies white dress & one shirt for myself I made Lizzie iron her dress & Aunt Chaney & I ironed the rest Mrs. Cheatam came to see me again to day & Katie too, heard that Mrs. May Stroud is rite sick Ella Chandler is sick too Lizzie is over there staying with Ella to night Aunt Chaney is here yet, I have felt better to day than I have this week, wrote to Miss Alfie to night am to send it to her by Brother Jim to morrow, got a letter from sister Bettie this evening. Fannie has been here twice to day she has a very sore foot, Fannie Archdale was here this evening the first time in a long time, Mr. Jackson & Mr. Morgan went over to Cousin Van's to day & Mr. Jackson took two trips out to

68. Anna Binson [*sic*] was born in 1860 in Arkansas. She was black.

night after supper. I dont know where he went nor what he done, he got some more coal oil yesterday & more sugar to day, 16 lbs, Fannie brought me some nice watermelon & I did enjoy it so much, Mrs. Chandler sent me a nice loaf of lite bread by Asher to day she also sent my table home she borrowed last sunday, Fannie sent me some nice fish & I ate them for my supper,

Sunday, August 10th 1890. Cloudy windy cool some warm some quite a different day to what to day four years ago was, Mr. Stillwell died just 4 years ago today & what a change what a change, Aunt Chaney & I went over to the McNiel grave yard & stayed a while then I came home & read some & took a nap have felt bad most all day, Aunt Emeline Davis sent me some nice peach cobler & some fried corn I did enjoy it so much Mrs Chiles, Mrs. Atkins Mrs Smithee & Fannie all came to see me today they did not stay long after they left & Mr. Jackson & I took a long walk around in the field, Ben Outlaw[69] came in & stoped a while, he is hunting work, Brother Dick & Brother Charlie went up to Mr. Morris' today Brother Dick borrowed a young horse from Mr Atkins & Brother Charlie rode Jim, they were both here for supper, Lizzie wrote to miss Carrie to day Aunt Chaney went to Emelines this morning & wont be back until tomorrow I feel better to night, gave Mrs Chiles & Mrs. Atkins some of the moss like what I have in a bucket hanging up,

Monday, August 11th. 1890. Clear & warm no rain yet Aunt Chaney washed for me & washed Brother Dicks satteen shirt & one under shirt I gave her 50 cents for what she done to day & what she washed Friday, she seemed very well pleased, Lizzie went down to Mrs. Howells to day & Sue came home, Mrs. H. was here a little while this morn-

69. Ben Outlaw was born in 1873 in Arkansas.

ing, I did some mending today Aunt Jane Osburn was here a while this evening Aunt Fannie Hurd too, Aunt Chaney went up to Uncle Jake Watsons & got me some peaches oh but they were nice so nice Brother Dick worked on the fense mr. Jackson cut & split a part of the big log that the water left in the yard, I went up to Fannies & stayed a little while late this evening the first time I have been there in over a week, Lizzie got a letter from her Cousin Mamie Caldwell this evening I opened & read it but have not sent it to her I have felt very well to day, Aunt Chaney killed one of my chickens I bought from Aunt Francis Hines & we had a part of it stewed with dumplings for supper & we are to have the rest fried for breakfast, Fannie has a very sore foot, she was down here a little while this morning, Ella Chandler is quite sick tonight Aunt Chaney went down to Henry Reeds to night but she is not coming back unless I send for her,

Tuesday, August 12th 1890, Cloudy some clear some & cooler windy still no rain have not done any thing to day but cook clean up & iron, washed Sue's head, she blacked the shoes for Mr. Jackson & Brother Dick he plowed for Dr. Chandler to day Mr. Jackson went to Red fork this morning & to Cousin Vans this evening, I have felt very well all day have been up to Fannie's twice to day she gave me a nice plate of venison steak for my supper Sue is at Mrs. Chandlers to night, got no mail to day, Cousin Van promised to come & cut the millet for Mr. Jackson yesterday but 2 days of this week have gone & he has not come yet, Will Emmit[70] rode Frank to day he is one of old Bettie's colts Mr. Jackson borrowed a peck of meal from Mr. Morgan today, I made some molasses cakes to day but they were not very good, Aunt Chaney went away last night she is not to come back unless I send for her, she stoped in a few minutes late this evening to see how I felt,

70. Will Emmit cannot be identified, but he seems to be a laborer who works around in the community as Ed Gordan does.

Wednesday, August 13th 1890. Cloudy some clear some & north wind still blowing some warmer to day Mr Jackson & Brother Dick did no work to day, oh yes Mr. Jackson plowed the sweet potatoes late this evening, he went down the road with Mr. Morgan this morning he has not done any thing much to day, I went up to Fannies this morning & then on over to see Mrs. May Stroud she is *very* sick, she is no better to night but I cant go set up with her, her mother & sister have come to stay with her, I cut & almost made Blanch White a lawn dress skirt to day she sent me a nice mess of corn today & I did enjoy it so much I feel so bad to night

Thursday August 14th 1890 Cousin Van cut the hay I was sick all day no rain Aunt Chaney washed a few things today. I went up to Fannie's once today I finished Blanches dress today.

Friday August 15th 1890. I had a hard chill sick all day. Lizzie come home this evening rode behind Alec on Pomp Mrs. Mary Stroud is no better. Mr. Burnet and Miss Ruth came down this evening. Sue went to Mrs. Giffords and Lizzie to Mrs Chandlers to stay all night. Dr and Mrs Chandler was here this evening and gave me calomel. no rain and Mr Jackson raked his hay today he had to go to Mr Irbys[71] to get the rake

Saturday August 16th 1890 Mrs Stroud is no better Mrs Cheatam came to see me and the baby today no rain Mr Jackson finished hauling his millet hay today the wild hay was too green to cut. Blanche came after her dress and paid for it to night. I am still very sick and have to take more medicine Mr Jackson has to sit up with me to night Mrs. Chandler and Miss Joe came down to see me this evening.

71. Albert Zedekiah Irby was born in 1858 in Georgia. He was married to Mary Coopwood, daughter of Benjamin Coopwood.

Fannie and Miss Ruth came down and stayed a while this evening. Mrs Smith sent me some okra and greens for my dinner. I ate it and enjoyed it so much. Mrs Chandler and Dr brought me a fine boy it's name is Davie Samuel Mrs Cheatam and Fannie named him we will call him Davie paid Aunt Emeline Davis 50 cts for washing.

Sunday August 17th 1890[72] Clear some, cloudy some, and very warm all day. Mrs Stroud is no better Mama was heap worse last night but is better tonight. Mama had a heap of company today. the baby is getting along fine and very good so far. Mama has been so sick ever since Thursday night we have had to sit up with her every night and give her medicine.

Saturday, August 23rd. 1890 Clear and some cooler, have been in bed a week; have had a heap of company this week, none yesterday except Fannie, Mrs. Chandler was too sick to come yesterday the baby has done well all the time except a little sick wednesday, Mr. Jackson stayed away all day wednesday & more than half the day thursday Fannie has stayed with me 4 nights Mrs. Smithee one but she did not sit up to do any good, the widow Smith set up all night sunday night. Mrs May Stroud died monday the 18th poor May I will never get to see her again in this life, Mrs. Cheatam has been to see me 3 times since I got sick Aunt Emeline Davis has washed for me twice & done one regular washing besides I have only paid her 50 cts Aunt Chaney & Lizzie done one small washing tuesday, Sue ironed one of Aunt Chaneys grandchildren is very sick & Anna sent for her yesterday & she could not come back Lizzie & Sue cooked dinner & supper yesterday & got on very well, Will Emmit came here to work thursday he has milked twice the children got breakfast & churned & cleaned up in the kitchen

72. This entry in a different hand was obviously made by one of the daughters.

61

& waited on me & got it all done before nine oclock, Mr. Jackson got Lizzie a pair of gloves when he went to Redfork wednesday, he also got Fannie a satteen dress Aunt Chaney a calico dress & Mrs. Chandler a dress & me some lemons, Lizzie got a letter from Miss Carrie thursday & answered it yesterday & sent it off this morning she has also written to Mrs. Jane Mask this week, I have got no mail all the week except a few papers, & I cant read them now, Mr. Jackson got Miss Ida Howells picture this evening Mrs. Wilson in Fla, sent it to him paid Aunt Emeline Davis 50 cents this evening for washing she has done for me this week, also let her have a 5 lb bucket of molasses, Sue washed some for the baby to day, Fannie has been here 3 or 4 times to day & Mrs. Chandler once Mrs. Chandler has been quite sick a gain this week, let Mr. Jackson have 25 cts I give Will Emmit yesterday & he got 25 cts for himself to day, he has bought me 10 cts worth of crackers since I been sick & some lemons, he brought 2 cans of peaches to the house for dinner yesterday I had a saucer full & he & the children ate the rest, Brother Dick went to the picnic out at Dumas yesterday & got back today Mr. Morgan went too so did Dr., Asher, Ed Gordan & Alex Hazel, they all got back before dark except Mr. Morgan & he did not get back until after dark, poor fellow he has been on a drunk & in a fight it is too bad, *too bad* I got no mail to day

Sunday, August 31st. 1890. Clear & pleasant windy some I have got on well all this week have been setting up some every day for a week, Mrs. Cheatam was here & spent the day last sunday & brought me some more butter I paid her a dollar & she owes me another pound yet, let Mr. Jackson have 50 cts for Will Emmit Friday, & yesterday let him have a dollar to pay Billie Lee[73] for work he done Sue took ten cents tuesday & got Aunt Chaney some smoking to bacco, Aunt Chaney went a way wednesday & has not been back

73. William Lee was born in 1854 in Mississippi. He was black.

since, Lizzie & Sue have done the cooking & Will Emmit the milking, they have all got on very well Lizzie has been up to Mrs. Smiths twice this last week & got me some greens

[September 1890]

Monday Sept. 22nd. 1890, Cloudy & rainy all day Miss Carrie came to board to day, Miss Fannie Owen is with her, Miss Sallie & Mr. Will[74] came to see us & stayed about 2 hours their baby is so pretty, Lizzie is some better I went up to Fannies & she & I baked a jelly cake for Lizzie, Aunt Francis Hines was out today & I wrote a letter to Anna for her,

Monday, Sept. 29th. 1890. Cloudy cold & rainy Lizzie is still improving but she cant go to school yet Miss Carrie Kate McNiel & I have nearly got her hair combed out, oh but it is such a task, Mr. Jackson went to Redfork this morning to get some pipe for the school house stove but got none he bought Lizzie Sue & I some handkerchiefs but I dont like them, there is too many colors about them, I bought 45 cents worth of beef from Prince Coalman[75] & paid for it, I sent Lizzie to the store Friday & she got me a dollars worth of cotton checks to make me some aprons I cut & made me one & to day I cut the rest in 2 aprons for her & she & I partly made one Mr. Jackson sold Reddie Sue's cow to Mr. Emerick for $14,00 dollars, he sold her tuesday or wednesday of last week, he gave the money to me & I have put away 10 dollars of it & had the other five changed so as I can use it, I got a paper dollar from Miss Carrie last week & I am going to pay for my Guide[76] some time soon

74. Miss Carrie was the teacher. Miss Fannie Owen and Mrs. Will Watkins (Miss Sallie) are her sisters.
75. Prince Coalman was born in 1837 in Arkansas. He was the son of Caroline Coalman and the son-in-law of Frances Hines. He was black.
76. The *Apostolic Guide* was a journal published in Kentucky by the Disciples of Christ from 1869 to 1907.

[October 1890]

Saturday, October 4th 1890 Clear & bright & cool but warmer than it has been, we have had some very cool unpleasant weather this week, Mrs. Coopwood[77] died tuesday night & was buried thursday. & mrs Brogan lost 2 of her children this week, one tuesday & one thursday, Mrs. Archdale came to see me yesterday the first time in about 4 months I have made some nice fresh yeast this week & had lite rolls 3 times I had good luck with my bread I cooked some to day for the folks to take out to the basket dinner tomorrow on the ridge, Mr. Jackson bought 8 hams thursday evening & I cut one & fried some for supper & then he took the rest of that ham to Fannie. Mr. Jackson got Sue a pair of shoes today & 2 pairs of pants for himself he has gotten 2 pairs of boots for himself since the 16th of August,

[November 1890]

Friday November 7th. 1890. Clear & hazy & warmer than it has been, we are all well today except Davie he had the colic rite bad all the morning he seems alrite now, just 2 weeks ago tonight I got a letter from Miss Alfie Edington, & it will be 2 weeks to morrow since I got a letter from sister Bettie Miller, Mrs Sallie Watkins is quite sick & has been for over a week. Miss Carrie went up there just a week ago to day & she is there yet. Miss Fannie taught this week in Miss Carries place, Sue went up to Miss Sallie's behind Miss Carrie & Miss Fannie brought her home Saturday & I let her go behind Miss Fannie again this evening for company for Miss Fannie, I made her a new gown & a new apron since yesterday morning, Miss Fannie went down & stayed all night with Annie Chiles last night, Miss Carrie paid me her board the 22nd of October & I have spent it all spent 2 dollars & a half for sweet potatoes

77. This is Mrs. Benjamin Coopwood.

Thursday, Jan, 1st. 1891. Cloudy cool & windy very windy we got up late, after breakfast was over we all went up to Mr. Coopwoods to a dining & spent the day Mr. Jackson Sue, Lizzie, Asher, Harry, & I, & baby all went in the wagon & Miss Carrie went too she rode Denmark her horse we all enjoyed the day so much, Asher stayed to come home with Miss Carrie Harry came home with us we got home 15 minutes after six, it is much colder to night than it was this morning; we all sat up last night until the old year died & the new year came, the children all enjoyed the candy stew last night & I think all went away satisfied. Just nine months a go to day I was at Mrs. Coopwoods & spent the day & Mrs. Coopwood was living & now she is gone, been dead just 3 months last night, Brother Dick came home tuesday night, & he went up to Mr. Coopwoods to night after we came home he rode George the mule got no mail,

Friday, Jan 2nd. 1891. Clear & cold & windy, we got up late this morning but I got breakfast in time for Miss Carrie & the children to get off to school, Caroline Coalman came & helped me get dinner & washed the babies things for me & Fannie & I went to see Mrs. Caulk & tell her good bye for she leaves tomorrow on the boat she was at Mrs. Giffords & we went there, Lizzie went up to stay all night with Katie McNiel & after supper Mr. Jackson & I took the baby & went to Mrs. Giffords & stayed 2 hours, & sue washed the supper dishes & Brother Dick stayed with her, after she got done she wrote to Eddie Mann, & Brother Dick wrote to Ella Chandler, Dr. Chandler went home to day,[78] Eddie Peoples[79] came after Miss Carrie & she went out to Mrs. Peoples to stay until sunday evening all well to night, no

78. The Chandlers seem to have moved to Walnut Lake sometime between October 1890 and January 1891.

79. J. Edward S. Peoples was born in 1876. He was the son of Dr. S. J. Peoples of Red Fork.

mail to day, Mr. Jackson & Brother Dick picked cotton today & Will Emmit too, John Hornbuckle was here awhile this morning,

Saturday Jan. 3rd 1891 Clear & bright & cold got a little work done today Lizzie ironed for me sent Mr. Jacksons 2 shirts to Victoria[80] to iron for me Brother Charlie came to day & stayed a good while Fannie came & stayed a while too, Katie McNiel is here to night with Lizzie & Sue, I paid Aunt Emeline Davis 50 cts for washing & let Mr. Jackson have a dollar to pay will Emmitt he gave me 50 cts, all well to night no mail except a paper, Lizzie cut & pealed the citron mellon & I put it in sugar I am going to cook it to morrow,

Sunday, Jan, 4th. 1891. Clear & cool big frost last night Fannie was here a while to day & I was up there a while Mrs. Gifford & Miss Josie came & stayed a while this evening, Brother Jim came to see us & stayed a while to day he looks bad because of last night, Miss Carrie came home this evening she said she had a nice time, Katie McNiel did not go home until late this evening, I wrote Mr. Wiggs a letter to night have just heard that Mr. Sam Hornbuckle[81] is worse he has been sick 3 weeks tomorrow, Ben Outlaw came here to day after some mustard for Mrs. Hunley she is quite sick, Brother Dick has gone to sit up with Mr. Hornbuckle,

Monday January 5th 1891 Clear & cold, Mr. Sam Hornbuckle died this morning before sunup poor man he suffered a great deal before he died I went up there after dinner & stayed a while Alex Hazel carried the baby across the foot log for me & up the road above Mr. Dyers horse lot & I went the rest of the way by my self, poor Mrs Hornbuckle she is so deeply grieved over the death of her son, the two

80. Victoria Lee, wife of William Lee, was born in 1864 in Mississippi. She was black.

81. Sam Hornbuckle, born in 1859 in Arkansas, was the son of Martha Hornbuckle.

sisters take it hard too Mr. Jackson & I are going up there after supper & sit up Lula Reed washed for me to day she got done before twelve oclock. I paid her 50 cts I have not done any work to day Miss Carrie taught school to day the children are well & went to school, Fannie Morgan & Nellie Smithee went down to sit up with Mrs Hunley she is no better, got no mail to day but an Ark City Journal Mr. Brown was here for a few minutes to day so was Cousin Nan, Aunt Lucinda Black sent me 16 lbs of butter to sell for her & I fear I am going to have a bad time selling it, Mr. J. & Will Emmitt hauled cotton to the gin to day, Brother Jim came down & told us all good bye this morning before he left

Tuesday Jan 6th. 1891. Clear some cloudy some & still rite cool, Mr. J & I set up at Mrs. Hornbuckles last night came home before day this morning & he laid down & took a nap & I churned & cooked breakfast & I had it ready before daylight, Mr. J. & Will Emmitt went to hauling cotton & I got the house cleaned up by the time the children had to go to school they helped me a good deal, I put out both feather beds in Miss Carries room & all the bedclothes & they got a good airing to day, I also ironed some to day & went up to Mrs. Hornbuckles & stayed a few minutes got the material & came back to Fannies & she helped me make the pillow & face cover,[82] & then came home & got dinner Brother Charlie came this evening but he did not stay very long he brought Mrs. Watson & Mrs. Morris down they went to Mrs. Dyers, Mrs. Morris went back but Mrs. Watson is at Mrs. Giffords, Mrs. G. was here to day she bought 2 lbs of the butter Aunt Lucindy sent here & I gave her a pitcher of butter milk, Fannie Morgan saddled her horse & started to go to the burying but did not go for she felt too bad I have not slept any to day have felt rite bad all day Brother Dick went after the coffin & he went to the burying Mr. Morgan went to help dig the grave Miss Carrie & Asher

82. These things are for Sam Hornbuckle's coffin.

took a ride this evening, Miss Sallie has come back from Pine Bluff, Aunt Chaney came & told us good bye I do hate to see her go away, Mr. Sample brought the other meat 2 hogs & Mr. Jackson cut the bones out & fixed it to cool oh but I did get so cold holding the lamp & he got mad at me because I would not tell him what Miss Carrie & I were talking about the other night

Wednesday, Jan 7th. 1891. Cloudy cool & rainy, oh but I did feel so awful bad this morning when I got up but I managed to get breakfast & Caroline came & helped me to clean up & get dinner & Victoria Lee came & helped me all day she & Caroline cooked the lard & ground the sausage & cleaned the heads & feet. & put them to soak to make souce, Caroline had to go home but Victoria stayed & helped me get through with supper & all, I got sick about elevin o clock & oh I was so fearful sick until about 3 I had such a terrible headache & was so sick at my stomach but I am better to night Miss Carrie combed the childrens heads for them to day, Judge Pindall came this evening & is here to night I sent Lizzie to the store yesterday & got a half gallon of coaloil & paid for it & I wrote an order there to day for sage & a broom got the broom but no sage wrote to Aunt Francis Hines mother to night Mrs. Hunley is no better, Lula Gifford was here today & got some swet milk & brought me a ten pound bucket her ma gave me, I got no milk atal yesterday for the calves got it all & I only got the milk from two cows to day, Mr. J & Brother Dick & Will Emmit sacked seed & hauled seed & cotton to day, John Henry was here a while to day so was Ella Davis, Joe came back yesterday he said all was well, I had to go to Fannies last night & get some bread for Will Emmits supper, Fannie was here a while to day while I was so sick, I got no letters to day

Thursday, January 8th 1891 Cloudy & cold & rainy, have not done very much today got all the lard dried up & put a

68

way & Victoria ironed the plain clothes for me & helped me get supper, I did a little mending this evening Miss Carrie did not get any letters to day neither did I all well tonight the baby has been tolerable good to day Mr. J. & Brother Dick hauled cotton seed & Will Emmitt cut wood & milked & did odd jobs, Judge Pindall ate dinner at Mr. Dyers to day & then went away, Aunt Chaney stoped this morning & told us all good bye, Aunt Emeline & her have gone to Pine Bluff to live, so has Aunt Louisa Cobb

Friday Jan 9th 1891 Cool cloudy & rainy, all well this is the last day of Miss Carrie's school & they are having a candy pulling at the school house & some of the children had speeches I did not care to go I have got a little work done this evening, cooked my souce to day Victoria washed some for me to day Nellie Smithee was here a while to day & I helped her to answer a note she got, Sue got a letter from Eddie Mann this evening, Mr. Jackson took a load of cotton to Redfork, & Brother Dick worked for Mr Dyer today & Will Emmitt did nothing but milk, cut wood & get a bout. Mr. Mayson Chiles [83] went home so drunk this evening that he was unable to drive his team he fell out of his buggy once & Mr. Morgan drove it for him & Mr. Jackson went too they got him home & put to bed then they came back & went to the candy pulling at the schoolhouse

Saturday Jan 10th. 1891 cool Cloudy & rainy, did no work but a little darning, washed Miss Carries head for her today she got a letter from Miss Sallie & got her cap & jacket, she also got a letter from Miss Alfie Edington, we got no letters today, poor Sue she has cried a heap to day because Miss Carrie & Lizzie are going away to morrow, Kate McNiel was here a while this evening I lent Nellie Smithee my shawl & Lizzie's bonnet for she & Fannie had to go down to sit up with Mrs Maggie Stroud & Bettie Hunley they are both

83. Mayson Chiles cannot be identified with certainty. However, he may be J. M. Chiles, who was a merchant and landowner in Watson in 1890.

sick Miss Carrie sent & bought herself a bottle of crystal cream & Lizzie got herself a bottle with the 25 cents Mr. Dick Jackson gave her for a Christmas gift, Dr. Chandler gave me a bottle & Sue a bottle & Mr. Jackson bought a bottle Victoria brought home the clothes she ironed them, all for me she also washed some for me yesterday, Asher Morgan went to Dumas to day with Mr. Mayson Chiles

Sunday, Jan. 11th 1891 Cloudy cold & rainy, Miss Carrie & Lizzie left today[84] they did not go until after dinner, oh but I did hate so bad to see them leave Brother Dick drove the wagon & took Miss Carrie's trunk & Lizzie & the valise with some clothes in it for Lizzie Sue went too they did not get back until after dark, Miss Carrie went away & forgot her pecans, oh but the room looks so empty since she left, I did hate it so bad because I could not fix a real nice dinner for them to day but we got up so late & it was long before I got the house cleaned up I did not have the chance to clean & fix chickens for a pie Mrs. Hornbuckle came this evening & stayed about 2 hours I was real glad to see her, poor dear soul I feel sorry for her, John Hornbuckle was here & stayed a while this evening, Fannie & Nellie came back this morning & said the sick folks were better,

Monday, Jan, 12th. 1891 Clear & bright when we first got up but by nine oclock it was cloudy & cold oh so much colder than it had been, I washed to day for the first time in nearly 6 months I feel very well to night Sue helped me, Fannie came down twice today Brother Charlie came & got the blanket & quilt of his that was here, Brother Dick helped Mr. Allen to moove Mr. Dyer up on the Ayers place to day. Mr. Jackson got John Hornbuckles horse to day & also let him have Jim to carry the mail on John gave him 50 cts for

84. Miss Carrie is going to Pea Ridge to board in the house of Joseph H. Jones and teach the school there. Lizzie is apparently going with her to get the benefit of both sessions of school. Pea Ridge is six miles away. Although there are no records about the school from 1890, the school roll for 1901 shows seventeen pupils, ranging in age from six to twenty.

the use of Jim & $2,00 two dollars for going in the woods & getting his horse, it snowed some to day but not enough to do much harm, dont feel like doing much work to night, oh but Miss Carrie & I did have such a hard time night before last night for the pup whined & the baby had the colic & cried lots I was up nearly half the night & had to give him Paragoric twice, I was sorry for it was the last night she was to stay with us, in a long time & it seemed like every thing tried to make a racket & keep her a wake

Tuesday, Jan 13, 1891. Clear & bright & cold, helped Fannie on her basque but we did not get it done Brother Dick borrowed Mr. Allen's horse & I went down to see Mrs. Hunley & stayed about an hour found Mrs. Stroud up & alrite & Mrs. Hunley better but still very sick, I sent her some sausage by Bell Young I got home before 3 oclock & got dinner & by that time it was night so I have done no work, sue took in the clothes & washed the dishes, Lula Gifford came & stayed a few minutes & I gave her some sweet milk Fannie has been down twice to day I helped her cut & fit her basque & to night she came & got some cotton, silk thread & perfume powder to make her some little perfume bags Sue went home with her to stay alnight, Lizzie got a letter from Mrs. Jane Mask & I opened & read it, Fannie took care of the baby & Sue, while I was gone Mr. Jackson has taken the mail for 3 months he carried it to day himself he made a bargain with Will Emmitt to night for him to work for Mr. Jackson at (8,00) eight dollars a month for 3 months, Will Emmitt & Brother Dick stretched some wire on the lane fense to day that & getting some wood is about all they have done Mr. Jackson rode George the mule to day

Wednesday, Jan 14th 1891 Clear & bright until about 9 oclock when it got warmer & clouded up & is cloudy to night. Fannie came down & we got her basque done all but the hooks & eyes & sewing in the sleeves & she took it

71

home & is finishing it to night, she got a letter from Ella today & she is going out to see her ma tomorrow she is going with Mr. Brown, Sue washed some for the baby to day & she cleaned up all the dishes, I wrote a note to Miss Carrie & sent it & 2 letters to her & one to Lizzie sent them all by Mr. Morris, oh but my left breast is swollen so bad to night & it hurts me, Mr. Jackson & Brother Dick worked on the log house in the field Mr. J. is feeling so very bad to night Will Emmit took the mail out to day & rode Jim horse Mr. Jackson put me up a nice shelf this morning at the window for my flower boxes

Thursday, Jan, 15. 1891 Cloudy & rainy all day Sue & I ironed up the clothes & I patched & mended up most every thing Will Emmitt carried the mail today & rode George the mule Mr. Morgan came down & set for about 2 hours with us to night & I gave him the note to take to Pendleton to morrow to collect for me Mr. Jackson got a letter from Brother Jim & I answered it to night & Sue wrote to Eddie Man, it rained so much Mr. Jackson could not work today, so he & Brother Dick done no work, we weighed the baby to night & he weighs 24 pounds, my breast is better to night, Mr. Jackson is better too

Friday, Jan, 16th. 1891. cold cloudy & rainy but fine misty, not all day Sue & I cleaned up the house & scoured the kitchen & seeded the raisins & baked a cake & Brother Dick borowed Mr. Allen's horse, 'Sam,' & went up on the ridge after Lizzie & Miss Carrie & they came & oh we were all so glad to see them, I baked 10 biscuits for Brother Charlie this morning & he paid me 15 cents, I sent Sue to the store & got 50 cts worth of coffee & paid for it Mr. Jackson took the mail out to day & rod Jim, Lizzie & Sue got a letter from their cousin Mamie Caldwell today. Mr. Morgan went to Pendleton to day, Mr. Jackson hired Billie Lee to cut & haul some wood to day

Saturday, Jan 17th. 1891. Cloudy & cold all day Miss Carrie & all of us set up late last night eating Pecans & raisins Brother Dick bought the raisins & Miss Carrie furnished the pecans & to day Miss Carrie & I borrowed Mr. Allens cart & went up to Redfork to see Miss Sallie she is living at Redfork now she & the baby are getting well now, we had a fearful cold muddy trip & Miss Carrie got so cold she was sick for a while after we got back, Lizzie & Sue had supper most done when we got home, they are up at Fannie's to stay alnight Mrs Smithee went out to Dr. Chandlers to day with Alex, Mr. Jackson took the mail to day & rode Jim, we got no mail except a paper I have not had any milk to day the cows did not come, oh my the week is gone & I have not done any work hardly

Sunday, Jan 18th. 1891. Clear & bright & pleasant not quite as cold as it was yesterday Lizzie & Sue cleaned up the house for me & Miss Carrie & I went up to Fannies & stayed about 2 hours, Miss Carrie has had headache all day, Fannie let me have a few slices of beef for dinner I came home got dinner & then Mr. Jackson borrowed Mr Giffords buggy harness & got Mr. Allens cart & hitched George the mule to it & Brother Dick took Lizzie up in the cart & Miss Carrie rode her horse Denmark, I put her Pecans in a sack, also some of the cake for their lunch tomorrow, I gave Lizzie the 50 cts to pay for her washing, have been here all evening with just Sue & the baby & Sue has been out playing with Harry & Willie Sue washed the dinner dishes for me, & then went over to Mollie Maysons & ground me some coffee Uncle Mat Stroud came over to day he is at Fannie's to night, Fannie went down to see Mrs. Howell this evening she said the sick folks were better, Mr. Jackson & baby & I went over to Mrs. Giffords & stayed about 2 hours, Sue had a chill to day & she stayed at home Brother Dick stayed with her he got home a little after 6, oh but it is lonely when Miss Carrie & Lizzie are away

Monday, Jan 19th. 1891 Clear & bright & warmer washed to day, Mr. J. took the mail rode George & brought the shepard pup home, Brother Dick & Will Emmit put strips on the shed room now it is more comfortable, Anna Binson was here today so was Uncle Mat he wanted to sell me his cow but I dont want to buy her, Aunt Francis Hines was here too she did not stay long, I went up to Fannies & ground some coffee for Sue is still sick she has taken 3 pills to day & I think has had another chill, wrote a letter to Charles H. Lowen, Nashville, Tenn. for Mr. Jackson to night let Mollie Mayson have a pound of butter for a dozen eggs

Tuesday Jan. 20th, 1891. Cloudy & warmer than yesterday Mr. Jackson took the mail & rode George, Brother Dick has not done any work to day Will Emmit dug some post holes & cut some wood I cut Lizzie's dress that her cousin Charlie gave her I want to make it this week, Sue has been in bed most all day, I think she has missed her chill to day I got a letter for Aunt Francis hines this evening, Caroline Coalman was here to day, gave her some yeast & some papers have not done very much work to day, got the henhouse cleaned out, it is raining some to night, have been up to Fannies twice to day Mr. Jackson has a very sore throat, Brother Charlie was here a while to day, Nellie & Alex came back to day & Nellie came down here & stayed a good while she brought sue some things Ella Chandler sent her for her doll,

Wednesday Jan, 21st. 1891 Cloudy & cold, cleared up late this evening & is clear to night & some warmer, Sue has been up today all day but she dont feel very well Mr. Jackson's throat is no better, he took the mail again to day & rode George, Jim got out of the field & went to the woods. & Will Emmit went out & got him today that & cut wood is about all he has done, Brother Dick did some work for Mr. Jackson tore down a cotton house & hen house I got Lizzies dress about half done went to the store & got 4½ yds of cotton flannel & Fannie hemed the baby 6 diapers, I got 18 yds of calico, three kinds to make a comfort, & a quarters worth of thread I churned to day for the first time this week did not make very much butter, let Mrs. Gifford have some butter milk & a little sweet milk she came to see me this evening & set a good while Mai came with her I have been to Fannie's twice to day, Mrs. Bettie Newby is quite sick to night, Lon Howell brought my syringe home this evening, Brother Dick has gone down to see Miss Annie Chiles to night

Thursday. Jan. 22nd 1891 Clear & bright & cold all day, Mr. Jackson took the mail to day & rode the horse he bought from Dove Newby, Brother Dick & Will Emmit did no work until after one oclock then they hauled some pickets to put on the fense I went up to Fannies & paid Mr. Morgan for the cow 'Cherry," ($12.50) twelve dollars & a half she is sue's cow. I milked her this morning, I sent Sue to the store & got $5,00 five dollars to pay Aunt Lucindy that is all I owe her, I sent money sack & cloths all by Marshal Stroud,[85] Tony Brooks was here a while to day Mr. Jackson's throat is very sore yet he had Dr. Austin to burn it with caustic but it is no better yet, I cut out some work to day, for myself I cut 2 gowns 2 aprons & 2 chimies, 2 pair drawers for Lizzie, 2 gowns, 2 undershirts for the baby Brother Charlie came & got his trunk & toolchest this evening, Sue & I ironed to day, Blanch White brought me the other eggs & I paid her for them & she took some things home to starch & iron for me & I am to give her some lite bread, Uncle Mat left to day

Friday Jan, 23rd, 1891. Cloudy & cold & rainy this evening & raining to night went up to Fannie's this morning & we went to the store & I got 4 yds of flannel & 4 yds of white lawn & 3 yds of embroidery all for the baby except enough of the lawn for an apron for my self, Fannie is going to help

85. Marshal Stroud was born in 1854 in Arkansas. He was black.

me sew some she made the babies dress to day I did some mending Mrs. Smith & her two children started down to see me but I was at Fannie's & they stoped there

Saturday Jan, 24th, 1891. Clear & cold made my quilt to day Brother Dick went up on the ridge to see Miss Carrie & Lizzie & take Lizzies dress to get it fit on her, & to take her a pair of shoes, Fannie brought the dress & both skirts home all finished they are so nice oh but I have had such a chill to day & am so sick to night,

Sunday Jan 25th. 1891 Clear & bright & cold Fannie came & cooked breakfast for me, & then went out to see her Ma Mr. Morgan took her Ione Howell & Willie they went in Mrs. Howells double buggy Mr. Jackson went to the Allen place to day & got a horse for himself, Mrs. Gifford & Bettie Newby came to see me this evening & stayed a while I have had to spend this day in bed to day is Mrs. Sallie Watkin's babies birthday it is a year old to day Mr. Morgan got $5,00 five dollars & give Fannie for to get me some things out at Walnut Lake,

[February 1891]

Wednesday. Feb. 11th. 1891 Cloudy all day the sun came out just a little 2 or 3 times, cool but not as cold as yesterday, it was a bright cold day & I washed for the first time in 3 weeks the week I was sick Mrs. Smith washed for me & Mr. Jackson paid her in meat, & last week Victoria washed & ironed for me & I paid her the money. I sent by Will Emmitt & got her a bottle of snuff which was 25 cts & then Sue went down there & took her the other 25 cents to day, Sue & I ironed today & I have had to milk every day this week & one day last week. Mr. Jackson is building a house for Mrs. Porter she came Sunday & has been here every night since, Will Emmitt has carried the mail every day this week & rode Jim. I have not done any sewing this week except

76

mending I made the baby one flannel & one white shirt last week & made a pair of pillow cases & a pair of drawers for Lizzie & finished her dress, & sent them to her sunday by Brother Dick. I also wrote to Miss Carrie & Lizzie & Lizzie wrote me a few lines, I hope Lizzie can get here before Cousin Mamie[86] leaves for I want her to see Lizzie, today is Willie Morgan's birthday he is 6 years old to day, Mr. & Mrs. Chestine were here a while to night,

Thursday, Feb. 12th 1891 Cloudy & drizly all day Cousin Mamie & Mr. Jackson & Robert all got off early this morning & Sue & I milked & cleaned up & then I took Sue & the baby to Fannie's & she took care of them & Nellie & I went down to Mrs. Howells & got 2 sacks of greens, oh but they are nice we had lots of fun going down & coming back, she rod pomp & I rode Selim, I almost made Lizzie's drawers & begun my gown. Mr. Jackson got the house nearly done to day

Friday, Feb. 13th 1891 Clear some cloudy some & warmer than it has been I finished the gown & drawers to day & milked. Cousin Mamie left for home to day Mr. Jackson got the house done she paid him $20,00 twenty dollars,[87] she also paid Mr. Winn the $5,00 five dollars that we owed for a colt, Brother Dick went up & brought Miss Carrie & Lizzie down oh but I am so glad to have them back home again Aunt Lucindy sent six lbs butter out today by marshal Stroud I gave him the dollar that I owed her for the 4 lbs she sent the 26th of Jan, I also sent her sacks home I sent Mrs. Cheatam a part of the greens I got at Mrs. Howells, I sent them by Will Emmitt he rode the mule to day he carried the mail yesterday & today & rode the mule yesterday I went to the store & got $10,00 ten dollars & had it charged

86. Cousin Mamie is the daughter of Mollie Caldwell, who is Mrs. Jackson's sister.

87. Presumably the "she" who paid Mr. Jackson was Mrs. Porter, not Cousin Mamie.

to Lizzie it is to pay for her board & a pair of overshoes Miss Carrie sent to Pine Bluff & bought for her, I will have to charge her with the stockings & gingham for her bonnet & handkerchiefs that Fannie got for her at Walnut Lake also 30 cent for silk elastic for garters, Mrs. Chestine was here a while today & I gave her some yeast Mrs. Newby has been here twice this week she bought the dinner bell, it is the one I bought from Miss Emma Branch last fall a year ago I gave 50 cents for it & she paid me the same, I gave her & Lula Gifford some fresh butter milk they were both here this evening, while I was at the store this morning I got a box of yeast powders 15 cents, a pound of black peper & I dont know what that cost & I also got a half gallon coaloil that was charged too all I got was charged

Saturday Feb 14th, 1891 Cloudy & cool, Will Emmitt took the mail & rode Jim, & Mr. Jackson took Denmark & the mule & went to Redfork & got some corn & brought Miss Fannie Owen & Miss Sallie Watkins & they are to stay with us until to morrow, oh but I am so glad to have them here & little Mollie Ashley is just as sweet as she can be, Lizzie & Sue said some of their speeches for Miss Sallie tonight & they have gone to stay with Mrs. Morgan we all went up there this evening & weighed, I sent for Victoria & she took the chickens home to dress & cook to morrow I got Lizzies cake made to day & worked the button holes in her over shoes & cook is all the work I have done to day Cam McNiel came to see Miss Carrie last night & stayed until late & then we all set up until eleven oclock & it is that again to night & we just fixing for bed,

Sunday Feb. 15th 1891 Cloudy & rainy & bad Victoria came & helped me to get breakfast & cleaned up & then came back & got dinner, & we had 14 for dinner besides Molly Ashley, Stonewall,[88] & Victoria today is Lizzie's 13th

88. "Stonewall" is the nickname for the baby, Davie. He is listed in the census for 1900 as "Stonewall" Jackson.

birthday, Mr. Frank Watkins,[89] Mr. Cam McNiel & Mr. Laurence Baldwin[90] were here for dinner they came to see Miss Carrie but were welcome all the same, Mrs. Fannie Morgan & Mrs Nellie Smithee & Willie Morgan were here for dinner, too, all seemed to have a plenty & to enjoy themselves too, Mr. Morgan & Harry went to Walnut Lake yesterday & came back to day & Asher came home too the teacher is a way & he came home while there is no school there, we have all had a pleasant day to gether Miss Carry & Lizzie did not go back this evening but stayed again to night Cam took Mrs. Sallie Watkins home, this evening, Miss Carrie hired Mrs. Giffords buggy for her to go in, Cam came & stayed a good while to night, Miss Fannie Owen is to stay a week with us,

[March 1891]

Sunday, March 1st. 1891. two weeks ago to day since I pened a line in here oh my what all has happened, oh so much that I cannever think of to put down, one thing certain I have not been able to do very much work the past 2 weeks & I have not been to Fannie Morgans in over a week, I had Rheumatism or Neuralgia in the back of my head neck & shoulders & I suffered a great deal, I did not do very much on the 16th of Feb. & in the evening Miss Fannie & I went over to Mrs. Giffords & stayed a while Miss Fannie got an invitation on the 16 to a dance to be over at Mrs. Frank Nadys,[91] on the 17th, she went, Cam took her in Mr. Allens cart, on the 17th I washed & mad starch & starched & that night I ironed my bonnet & the babies white dress thinking I was going to get to go up to see Mrs Sallie Watkins, but it

89. Frank Watkins was the brother of Will Watkins, Sallie's husband. They are both sons of Major William Watkins, a prosperous farmer at Red Fork.
90. Lawrence Baldwin was born in 1860 in Mississippi. He married Martha Lou Hornbuckle in 1898.
91. Frank Nady was born in 1833 in France. He was probably the most prosperous planter mentioned in the diary.

rained & I could not go, so Sue & I cleaned the yards some & burnt some of the trash & by the 19th I was hardly able to do any thing Miss Fannie came home from the dance Wednesday morning & slept some & that evening she went over & stayed all night with Miss Josie Gifford & the next day Miss Annie Chiles came after her & she went down & stayed all night with her & they came back Friday & it was raining most all day & that was the day Mr. Jackson hauled the logs to make us a smoke house & thc next day he put the most of the logs up, Judge Pindall was here for a few minutes that was the day he lost his satchel, that was a bright windy day, I had to send for Victoria to come & cook for I was not able, on Sunday I was no better, & she still cooked & cleaned up & that was the day Mr. Jackson went out to Walnut Lake after Mrs. Chandler & Ella & they came Monday which was the 23rd, they stayed just a week Mr. Jackson took them home to day & Willie Morgan has gone too, Dr. Chandler was out week before last & stayed alnight with us one night, it was the 19th this last week Victoria has cooked washed ironed & part of the time, milked, I had to get her to wash Lizzie some clothes saturday & she will wash for me again this week, I am a heap better, Mr. Jackson went to Redfork tuesday & got me some medicine from Col. Combs & it is doing me so much good he took Miss Fannie up to her sisters wednesday & Cam brought her back yesterday evening & she is to stay here for a while brother Dick went up after Lizzie & Miss Carrie Friday & they came & stayed until this morning & they all went up to church Mr. Allen lent Miss Fannie his horse to ride, Mr. Jackson went off yesterday morning & did not get back until after supper last night he brought us some nice beef Mrs. Chandler & Ella & Fannie came down & Lizzie said her speech for them, Mr. L Baldwin & Cam McNiel came last night & stayed a long time, Miss Fannie brought me the shoes that Mr. Frank Watkins ordered for me they are so nice, she got a pair & Miss Carrie got a pair, oh but Miss Sallie did send me such a nice treat some biscuits & meat some cake & pickles & some candy, on thursday of this last week Nellie Smithee burnt up 6 or 7 garments for Mrs Morgan she ironed for her & left the clothes near the fire & turned the chair over & let the clothes burn there was one skirt that belonged to Mrs. Chandler & 3 or 4 garments belonged to Nellie, I sent Lizzie to the store & got her 18 yds of cotton stripe to make her some new aprons & I cut one saturday & miss Carrie made it for me water still rising but not very fast

Monday March 2nd 1891. Cloudy & warm & windy cleared off about one o clock & was bright all evening, I went up to Fannies & she went to the store with me & I got 4 dollars in money & had it charged to me all so a dozen spools of thread, & 20 yds of unbleached domestic & had that charged to Lizzie I also got her a comb it is horn & bound with brass, I have not done very much work to day, Miss Annie Chiles came up this evening & Miss Fannie went home with her to stay all night, Mr. Jackson did not get home until nearly 8 o'clock, he brought me a nice lot of turnips & greens Mrs. Brown sent them, Victoria got breakfast & cleaned up the house

Tuesday, March, 3 1891 Cloudy rainy & windy after twelve it got colder I did no work except to help Mr. Jackson make back bands Victoria washed for me also for Miss Fannie she & Miss Annie went to Redfork horse back this morning, they got them some cheap calico dresses to make for a calico party they are to have at Miss Annie's thursday night Miss Fannie took the money to Red Fork & paid Mr. Frank Watkins $3.25 three dollars & twenty, I have let Victoria have 2 ten lb buckets of flour that is all I have paid her, she went up to Mrs. Morgans & got me a bucket of meal got it in the milk bucket,

Wednesday March 4. 1891 Clear & bright & cold, suned 2 beds & ironed the clothes & got dinner Miss Annie & Miss

Fannie made their dresses to day & Miss Annie stayed all night with Miss Fannie, I milked the cows this morning & Kate kicked at me with her foot tied up Lillie has not been up since last Friday, Eddie Alexander is carrying the mail for Mr. Jackson he begun the 24th of Feb. he rides Frank some Jim some & the mule some Billie Lee came home to day I made starch & starched all the clothes, Mr. Jackson went to Mr. Nadys to see if he would furnish us for the year & he says he will,[92] Nellie Smithee & Kate were here a while this evening, Nellie went back to Mrs. McNiels last week after she burnt the clothes at Mrs. Morgans

Thursday March 5th 1891 Cloudy & rainy all day Miss Annie went home about twelve oclock she went with Ramsy in the double buggy, they could not have the dance because it rained too much, I cut & made Lizzie a chimise & made her new bonnett to day water still rising, heard that Nellie has gone to Mrs. Newbys to live left Mrs McNiels to day, Mr. Jackson milked today

Friday, March 6th 1891 Cloudy all day rained some Miss Fannie put the triming on the babies & Lizzies bonnetts & on Lizzies shimise, & I made her an apron & pair of drawers Victoria washed some for the baby to day, Sue went up with Brother Dick after Miss Carrie & Lizzie & rode pomp, Mr. Jackson bought us some nice fish & we had a splendid mess for supper, the water is still rising it is nearly half way over the field Mr. Jackson got some sugar & invited a lot of the folks & they had a candy pulling & danced some but broke up at twelve o clock,

Saturday, March 7th 1891 Cloudy some & rainy, did not do very much work today Miss Carrie & Miss Fannie made

92. This means that Frank Nady will lend W. T. Jackson enough money for the family to live on and buy seeds and labor to make a crop. The crop, farm animals, equipment, and sometimes the land served as collateral. He will be repaid when the crop is harvested.

some more candy & it is so nice Miss Carrie wants to take some of it home with her. Lizzie took the baby up to Mrs. Morgans a while this morning, water still rising, Brother Dick took Miss Carrie & Miss Fannie boat riding this evening they could not go far because it rained, Mr. Jackson had to go to Redfork to see Judge Pindall, & did not get back until late, he went in the woods this morning & got Nell & her colt & Mary & put them in the lot up at Mrs. McNiels, I got no letters,

Sunday, March, 8th. 1891. Cloudy & rainy & colder cleared up some late in the evening & Mr. Jackson took Miss Fannie Lizzie & Sue boat riding & Brother Dick took Miss Carrie, I have been sick with cramp this evening, Miss Carrie & Lizzie are to stay until morning, Fannie Totten came here this evening & I let her have a dose of pills for Walter, Miss Carrie & Miss Fannie did not have any company to day but Cam Adie & Ed all here to night. Eddie & Adie dressed & blacked like darkies & we had lots of fun laughing at them,

Monday, March 9th. 1891 Clear & bright & cold Miss Carric & Lizzic got off alrite & I fixed them a big lunch sent up to Mrs. Morgan & got some butter so as I could butter them some bread I fixed to wash & Victoria came & helped me & we got done & I got dinner all by 2 o clock, Miss Annie Chiles was here & spent the evening & her Ma spent the evening at Mrs. Morgans Mr. Jackson finished the garden fense to day, Brother Dick took Miss Carrie & Lizzie to the school he got back about twelve o clock, water still rising, Sue had another chill to day let Mr. Jackson have the dollar that I had in the house belonging to Aunt Lucinda Black,

Tuesday, March 10th 1891. Clear & windy & warmer than yesterday, put out the beds in Miss Fannies room & she helped me & then she put up some pictures & I made starch, & starched the clothes & Mrs. Cheatam came & spent the day I got dinner & finished up some patching, I got Asher & Harry to go to the store for me & get me a dollars worth of coffee a dollars worth of sugar a half gallon coal oil & a box of capsules Miss Fannie cut & made Sues sateen that her Cousin Fannie gave her over a year ago, it is nice & will look well with the red calico waist & sleeves she is going to make for her to wear with it I wrote Mrs. Blidenburg a note & sent her yeast to her by Eddie he rode Mack the mule again to day, Mr. Jackson & Brother Dick went to the woods to float logs Mr. Morris went with them Mr. Morgan got Lizzie a pair of shoes to day. I like them I think they will last her a while

Wednesday, March 11th. 1891. Cloudy cold & rainy all day, milked the cow & got Emmit to feed her Mr. Morgan & Mr. Jackson put the calves & Mat across the bayou this morning, they marked & branded the calves yesterday Miss Fannie helped me iron to day, she did the most of it, Sue got a letter from Dr. Chandler to day & he sent her such a pretty dress in the mail, water water rose 4 inches from yesterday morning until this morning, Sue answered her letter to Doc Chandler & all so to Eddie Mann, Mr. Jackson & Brother Dick floated logs again to day Mr. Morris went too Brother Dick got wet he fell over board,

Thursday March 12th. 1891 Cloudy & rainy & cold some sleet tonight, I cut 4 garments for Lizzie to day & got one made the water is running through town & still rising Mr. Jackson was sick all the morning & did not do very much to day they put the cows all across the bayou Mr. Jackson milked for me to day Brother Dick helped John Hornbuckle to moove into the brown house to day

Friday March 13th 1891 Clear & bright & cold, I got another garment made & sent them & an apron & the shoes to Lizzie by Brother Dick he & Mr. Allen went up to the Pearidge church this evening to hear the children say their speeches, Mr. Jackson Mr. Morgan & Asher went up on the ridge to see about the stock & feed some of the horses, I have got the most of my mending done this week, Mrs. Morris came to see me this evening & stayed a long time & then Miss Fannie & I went up to Mrs. Morgans & stayed a good while, she was down here a while this morning, Cousin Van was here a little while this evening he let me read a letter that Aunt Mary Sims got from sister Mollie Caldwell, & one came to Lizzie to day from her Cousin Mamie & I answered it to night, the water is still rising [marginal note:] sent Aunt Lucindia the dollar I owed her by Marshal Stroud

Saturday, March 14th. 1891 Clear & bright & cold Mr. Jackson went to Redfork and was gone until dark, Mrs Hornbuckle & Miss Laura went over the river to day, Miss Fannie & I went up to Mrs Morgan's again to day & she gave me a mess of peas & I shelled them up there, I patched some today, got no letters the water still rising but not quite so fast Mrs. Smith & her 2 children went a way to day they are at Redfork waiting for the boat they have got to start to their home at last Brother Dick made me 2 plat forms for my water barrels today sent Sue to the store & got me some molasses a gallon he also made me a shelf across the other end of the galory for my flower boxes, just a year ago to day Fannie Morgans baby died.[93]

Sunday March 15th 1891. Cloudy & cold sun shone out some this evening, Mr. Jackson borrowed Mr Morris' wagon & got pomp from Mr. Morgan & took Sue & I & baby to see Mrs. Sallie Watkins & spent the day, enjoyed myself so much found Miss Sallie & baby well, Mr. Pointer preached at Redfork today but I did not go to preaching, Miss Fannie stayed with Mrs. Morgan she will go up to see Miss Sallie

93. This is the only mention of this tragedy in the extant section of the diary. The death of Fannie's baby may explain some of the solicitousness with which she is cared for in the early months.

tomorrow or wednesday, Brother Dick stayed at home all day sick & is rite sick now water not rising very fast

Monday, March 16th. 1891. Clear & bright, water only rose half an inch from yesterday morning until this morning I washed to day & got done before 2 o clock, Mr. Jackson went up on the ridge to see about the horses & feed Bettie, he brought Miss Lula Coopwood home behind him she has been sick but is better, brother Dick feels a little better to day, Miss Fannie & I went to the store this morning & I got me a dollars worth of soap twenty five cents worth of soda, & spent 25 cents for lining to fix Mr. Jacksons coat, & fixed one side & part of the other, I paid for the lining & the other things were charged, I also got 8 yds cotton stripes to make me some aprons that was charged too, I feel bad tonight the baby & I are taking a cold & have been sneezing so much the baby was weighed today & weighed 27 pounds he is seven months old to day the water is running around in front of the store since I was there this morning I was up at Fannies a while to night & she was here

Tuesday, March 17th. 1891 Clear & bright & cool, water still rising but slow, put out the beds in miss Fannie's room, fixed Mr. Jacksons coat & did some other jobs, Miss Fannie made the waist for sue to wear with her sateen, the dress Miss Sallie gave her, Miss Lula is here yet I dont feel any better to night I went up to Fannies this evening & she lent me Selem & I rode over to Mrs. Giffords & stayed a while May is sick but she is up & about Fannie went over there this morning & stayed a while I ate some turkey at Fannies & she sent some to Miss Fannie & Lula they went boatriding this evening Eddie & Adie took them, Mr. Stroud bought the turkey & gave it to Mrs Morgan it weighed 22 pounds dressed oh but it was fat & nice & I did enjoy it so much

Wednesday, March 18. 1891 Clear & bright some, cloudy some, Miss Fannie Owen went to see her sister Miss Sallie at Redfork & spent the day & Miss Lula went up to Mrs. Morgans & stayed all day & is there to night I dont feel any better Mr. Jackson floated logs to day, I suned the beds & did odd jobs all day, went up to Mrs. Morgans this morning did not stay long, the water still rising it is nearly to the henhouse Mr. Morgan went to Pendleton to day, sue is at Mrs. Morgans to night Cam McNiel gave us a large fish this evening

Thursday, March 19, 1891 Clear & pleasant, Mr, Jackson went up on the ridge & took Miss Lula Coopwood home & then worked some on the house he is fixing for a smoke house & kitchen, oh yes it was cloudy all morning the water is still rising but very slow, patched some to day & Miss Fannie & I went up to Mrs. Morgans & stayed a good while late this evening, the babies cold & mine are not very much better, he is better than I am, Bell Young gave me a nice mess of fish this evening. Will Emmitt ate supper here last night

Friday, March 20th 1891 Clear & bright & warm Miss Fannie cut & made Sue's satteen that Dr. Chandler gave her, she went up to Mrs. Morgans & made it on her machine I put a new back in Mr. Jacksons vest & did some more patching & darning, Mr. Jackson & Brother Dick went out after ash logs to day I put some dirt in boxes & had Sue to set out the shellot buttons Mr. Morris gave us, I also swept the yard some, the water is rising yet it is all around the hen house it is cloudy & threatening rain to night, Bell gave us another fish this evening, Mr. Jackson killed a coon & brought it home

Saturday, March, 21st. 1891 Clear & bright & cold & windy, I cut Sue's new hubbard & Miss Fannie took it & went up to Mrs. Morgans & made it that makes 4 new dresses for Sue & Miss Fannie has made them all. Mrs. Morgan was here a while this evening, I made an apron & a chimise for myself today, we had some rain last night Asher & Harry

87

got me 2 barrels of chips thursday yesterday I nailed up some boxes in Brother Dicks room & put up the sacks off the floor & all so my papers & then turned the bed around we are all better tonight Fannie heard from her ma to day they are all well but Mrs. Chandler when Mr. Morgan went to Pendleton I gave him the note to get me some money & to night he gave it back to me & said I had no money in Mr. Burnetts hands that I had been given credit for it on the books & that $13,00 dollars did not pay this last years account including what was made on the place may the Lord have mercy on us but I do hate so bad to think that all the childrens money is gone & they have got hardly half an education Mr. Jackson went to Redfork to day to take a bale of cotton he got us some navy beans

Sunday, March 22nd. 1891 Clear & bright & warm until very late then it clouded up & turned a little cooler, Mr. Jackson & Mr. Morgan went to the ridge to see about the horses, I went to Mrs. Archdales this morning & set a while Bill & Lee are both sick with Pneumonia after I got dinner Mr. Jackson took Miss Fannie sue & I a nice long skiff ride we went down to Mr. Atkins & stoped a while it is the first time I have seen Mrs. Atkins in a long long time she has a real nice looking baby, I wrote Lizzie a note & sent it by Brother Dick but he did not go any farther than the school house so he did not see them & I got no note from them I wrote a letter to John R. Ludwick to see if I can dispose of the old coins I have, & sent a stamp for a reply,

Monday, March 23rd. 1891. Cloudy some clear some & warmer than usual Mrs. Cheatam & Katie came down & stayed until about one o clock Mr. Cheatam took Mrs. Chestine home she lives on Mr. Mayson Chiles place, I washed to day Victoria came & helped me, she finished the washing while I got dinner Miss Fannie did not feel well & she laid down all the morning & this evening she went up & cut & fit Mrs. Morgans wrapper for her, she sent to Mrs. Molly

Watkins saturday & got the pattern for Mrs. Morgan Mr. Jackson brought it for her, I went to see the sick folks to day they are some better not much, I have not done very much work today the water is still rising it is in the yard almost to the back steps, Aunt Francis & her daughter Anna was here a little while Aunt Francis brought me 3 envelopes & stamps & 3 sheets of paper to answer her letter, I had to write a note to Miss Carrie to night so have not answered it I have been to Mrs. Morgans once today Mr. Jackson worked on the house some to day he has one side covered & mashed his finger & quit I got no mail to day Sue has gone to bed feeling so bad, Marshal Stroud brought me 3 lbs of butter Friday evening I still owe Aunt Lucinda the dollar & a half for he did not get the cloth as I supposed when he was here a week ago he said she gave me that but I will pay her for it,

Tuesday, March 24th 1891 Cloudy some clear some I helped clean up the yard some & try to save the boards & things that are apt to float away Sue helped all she could the water is under the house, & still rising it has not rained any hardly in 12 days & yet the water don't fall, Mr. Jackson & Mr. Morgan went up to look after the stock to day[94] & Mr. J took Miss Carrie the note for me & one for Miss Fannie & Miss Carrie & Lizzie wrote a few lines they have not decided whether they will come next Friday or not I have not sewed one bit to day, baby Stonewall is not so well he seems to have a little fever, I have been to Fannies 3 or 4 times to day Miss Fannie has been there all day sewing she has made little Molley Ashley 2 dresses to day calico with a red polka dot, Brother Dick went to the woods with Mr. Morris to day Bell Young gave me nice piece of fish to day sue seems alrite to night, I feel very well. Mr. Burnett has not come yet I do wish he would come & let us have a settlement, I made starch & starched 3 pieces for myself & 3 for Fannie & she

94. Mr. Jackson has apparently taken his stock to higher ground at Pea Ridge.

is going to iron Stonewalls white dress for me, I wrote to Aunt Francis Hines mother to night,

Wednesday March 25th. 1891. Cloudy most all day it rained a good eal last night the water is rising yet, it is almost all over the yard Davie Stonewall is not any better, I have done nothing to day but clean & cook & moove & fix things for the overflow, took every thing out of my pantry & Mr. Jackson fixed it & we put the chickens in there, I put the eating table in my room & the things out of the pantry into the kitchen Mrs Archdales sick folks are some better this evening I borrowed a 10 lb bucket of sugar from Mrs. Morgan & I also owe her a teacup of sugar I made Sue's birthday cake ready for to morrow, Brother Dick went with Mr. Morris in the woods to day Mr. Jackson went to Redfork to day & got us a pound of tea & a gallon of molasses Miss Fannie made 2 white peco dresses to day she was at Mrs. Morgans all day again to day Mr. Stroud let me have the book to day so as I could look over our account I am not as much in debt as I thought

Thursday, March 26th. 1891 Cloudy cool & windy washed some for the baby, picked a chicken & fixed it to stew for dinner, Bell gave me another big piece of fish I put the buttons & button holes on Mrs. Morgans new wrapper Miss Fannie helped her make, & went to see Mrs. Archdale's sick children they seem better, Mr. Jackson went up on the ridge to see after the horses & took Miss Carrie & Lizzie a piece of Sues birth day cake Sue is ten years old to day I sent Mr. Sledge[95] 2 hens by Eddie & he is to give me a dollar for them but he did not send the money by Eddie, I ironed to night & Miss Fannie helped me I was at Mrs. Morgans a little while late this evening Sue got a box of pretty flowers in the mail to day Brother Dick got some wood to day he & Mr. Jack-

95. This is Tom Sledge. After the 1892 floods, Tom Sledge, his wife Ada, and their daughter Eugenia moved to Alabama, where Eugenia married William B. Bankhead and became the mother of Talullah Bankhead.

son cut it for the fire place & piled it on the galery Mr. Jackson has set up with Bill & Lee Archdale a part of 2 nights & Brother Dick has stayed there almost all night 2 nights, the water is still rising but very slow it is a goodeal colder to night, we have some land out yet, Sue & I piled boards & pickets & other things up out of the water this morning, Stonewall is better, Sue is complaining some but nothing serious

Friday March 27th. 1891. borrowed 8 teacups of coffee from Mrs. Morgan today paid it back April 4th. 1891

Friday March 27th. 1891 Clear & bright, cool & cloudy in the morning but bright & clear, water still rising but very slow I went up to Mrs. Morgan's & stayed a little while I borrowed 8 cups of green coffee, I fixed Sue's aprons to day Brother Dick went after Miss Carrie & Lizzie & they did not get here until almost dark, the baby seems better to night. Mr. Allen came & stayed about two hours, I cooked the last of the beans to day, Lizzie did not send Sue the box of pretty flowers she got in the mail yesterday for a birthday present Miss Josie Gifford was here & stayed a long time this evening, Eddie brought me the dollar for the chickens Mr. Jackson put Charlie horse across the bayou this evening & in the gin on a scaffold, Mr. Scales helped him, I got Victoria to iron Brother Dicks white shirt & to wash & iron Eddies clothes for me,

Saturday, March 28. 1891 Clear & bright, water did not rise very much just the least little bit I made Lizzie's other apron to day & got up some quilt pieces for Miss Carrie, Miss Carrie Miss Fannie & Lizzie took a boat ride this evening, I went up to Fannies & then on over to see Mrs. Archdales sick children, Bill & Lee[96] are better but Fannie[97]

96. Bill and Lee Archdale were nineteen and fifteen, respectively.
97. Fannie must be another name for Bulah Archdale, who was twelve at this time, according to the census for 1880.

is sick now, Mrs. A. thinks she is just like Bill & Lee, I got Mr. Jackson to kill a chicken for me & I dressed it so as to have it for breakfast in the morning, Mr. Jackson went to Redfork to day & Brother Dick went in the woods with Mr Morris, Lizzie & Sue parched and ground me some coffee to day, the baby is better to night

Sunday. March 29th. 1891 Clear some cloudy some & very warm, the water almost to a stand, Miss Carrie & Lizzie did not go until after 2 oclock, Mr Lawrence Baldwin came to see Miss Carrie and was here for dinner, after Miss Carrie left Mr. Frank Watkins & Mr. Jack Furguson[98] came & stayed about 2 hours. & after they left Mr. Jackson took Miss Fannie a boat ride, when he went to feed the horses, Mrs. Morgan went to Mrs. Chile's & spent the day, I did not go anywhere for there is too much water to walk to Mrs. Morgans, I had to wade with my over shoes on yesterday when I went up there, so apart of the day has seemed lonesome to me, Mr. Jackson went up on the ridge today to see about the horses & to make smokes, the baby coughed a good eal last night but he seems to be alrite this morning & has seemed alrite all day Mrs. Nellie Smithee left to day trunk & all Mike & Alex took her in a dugout,

Monday March 30th. 1891. Cloudy cold & rainy all day the water still rising it begun to run through the yard to night by the Pecan tree, we have only a small spot of ground out in front of the house I washed to day had to set the kettle in the fire place to boil the clothes I had to stop to fix the lunch & did not get done until nearly 4 oclock, Sue had a chill this morning & has fever yet so I have had all the work to do, but Miss Fannie is good & helps me so much Mr. Jackson went to the ridge again today I gave Brother Dick a quarter & he went & got me some coaloil ten cents worth, John Hornbuckle is here to night with Eddie & Brother Dick is at Mrs. Morgans,

98. John R. Ferguson [*sic*] was born in 1866 in Mississippi.

Tuesday, March 31st. 1891 Clear & bright & cool, Sue is still in bed with fever sent to Redfork to day & got a bottle of niter & we are giving her calomel, I ironed to day & did some mending Miss Fannie helped me to iron & she mended nearly all of Eddie Alexanders clothes, Brother Dick & John Hornbuckle went down on old river to day they got back just after sundown, Mr. Jackson went in the woods with Mr. Morris I got a letter from Ella Chandler to day, Mrs. & Mr. Morgan was both here for a little while this evening so was Miss Annie Chiles she is staying at Mrs. Morgans this week, sent 25 cts to the store by Brother Dick & got 15 cts in stamps and a package of plane envelopes Mr. Jackson & Miss Fannie fixed up some April fools for Miss Josie Gifford they are going to send them to morrow, Mrs. Archdale sent Mr. Jass Baldwin here to day & got the blistering ointment that Mr. Peoples gave Mr. Jackson, water rising

[April 1891]

Wednesday, April 1st. 1891 Cool cloudy & rainy all day, Sue still in bed sick she has fever yet, Miss Fannie & Brother Dick had lots of fun sending April fools to day, but they did not get any, I set up last night until twelve oclock, I dont feel very well to night have not done much today but cook wait on Sue & the baby & do a little mending, Mr. Jackson & Brother Dick did no work to day except cut a little wood Sue got a letter from Dr. Chandler today & Lizzie got one from Mrs. Jane Mask. Mr. Jackson's time for carrying the mail is out & Eddie is to board here until John Hornbuckle gets home Mr. Jackson & Brother Dick brought Charley horse over this evening oh but he did cut a dash swiming John Hornbuckle is going to use him, to get him broke water rising yet but very slow, Brother Dick's board begins to day he will pay $7,00 seven dollars a month

Thursday. April 2nd. 1891. Cloudy & cold north west wind, cleared up late in the day about twelve oclock bright but cool the rest of the day, washed some this morning cut some quilt pieces for Miss Carrie Sue still in bed she ate some to day & set up nearly an hour but she has fever yet & we are giving her more calomel to night will have to sit up all night, Mrs, Morgan was here a while to day she brought me some grits & I cooked them & had them for supper, Eddie Alexander got Sue 25 cts worth of lemons to day I gave him the money to pay for them he did not take the mail any farther than Mr. Cheatams, Pete Willis took it the rest of the way, Miss Fannie has gone to Mrs. Giffords to stay alnight Eddie carried her over in a dugout, I wrote a note to Miss Carrie to night to send to her by Mr. Jackson to morrow, he & Brother Dick went to Mr. Nadys today water not rising so much as it did yesterday & the day before, there is land out at the wood pile yet but very little, Mr. Jackson is setting up but he is asleep Mr. J. has begun to practice writing & I think he will succeed

Friday, April 3rd. 1891. Clear & bright & cold & windy, made myself a cook apron did the house work as usual waited on Sue she is no better, I set up last night until half past 3. Mr. Jackson set up until 20 minutes to 2 & he set & slept the most of the time, I took a nap to day, Mr. Jackson went up on the ridge to see about the horses he took my note to Miss Carrie, Brother Dick went up to Mr. Coopwoods in a dugout & brought Lizzie home she walked down that far from the school Miss Fannie came home to day she has a severe head ache to night, Mrs. Morgan came down twice today she & I have swaped dresses, mine does fit me so nice & she has to make hers, when she & Miss Carrie was making her dress before Christmas I did not think I would ever own it, I like it so much. I got Brother Dick to go to the Store & get me $6,00 & I paid Mr. Morgan $2,50 two & a half for the shoes he got Lizzie, Sue dont seem any better to night, Mr. Jackson turned the cow & calf together to day & took them away so I gets no more milk for a long time, water still rising

Saturday, April 4th. 1891 Cold & windy but sunny & bright. Mr. Jackson went to Redfork to day he took Miss Fannie in the boat she has got to go see Miss Sallie twice lately, Sue seems to be some better to day she has had on her clothes & set up some Victoria was here a while to day I made her a bucket of yeast she brought the flour, I also paid her the two dollars I owed her, Brother Dick did not go any where to day he took me to the store & I saw Mr. W. H. Burnett & he & I have settled at last, & he windes me up I just had (21,50) twenty one dollars & a half coming to me, I did not have the rite papers & I had to come back & get them & Brother Dick took me up to Mrs. Morgans & after Mr. Burnett & I settled he brought me back Brother Dick & I ate dinner at Mrs. Morgans & after I came home, Asher & Harry came & took Lizzie up to Mrs. Morgans, I have not done any sewing to day, Miss Fannie & Mr. Jackson got home before sundown Mr Jackson got us a gallon of molasses, 3 dollars worth of coffee & I think he said 20 pounds of sugar, Mr. Morgan was here a while this evening, Sue does not eat much I got Mr. Jackson to kill another hen & I fried her 2 pieces she ate a little,

Sunday, April 5th, 1891. Clear & bright & cold, water still rising but we dont think it is rising very much today it has gotten very windy since yesterday morning it has been clear up till then, we have all stayed at home all day except late this evening Eddie took Miss Fannie & Lizzie out for a little ride, & Harry took Lizzie up to Mrs. Morgans & she ground me some coffee I also paid her the coffee I borrowed I still owe her the sugar. Mr. Jackson took Mack the mule to Mr. Charley Malpass[99] he is going to keep him until the water goes down & Mr. Jackson fixed a place up in Mrs. McNiels lot for Jim out of the water he cut some wood late this evening, Annie Chiles is up at Mrs. Morgans again to night,

99. Charles S. Malpass was born in 1845 in Arkansas.

Sue has set up some to day & had on her clothes all day she seems better but she does look so bad, Brother Dick went up on the ridge today but he did not go to see Miss Carrie but he had a good time all the same, Eddie left this evening Mr. Jackson lent John Hornbuckle 3 pounds of meat, the water is falling,

Monday, April 6th. 1891. Clear & bright & windy not quite so cool as yesterday Lizzie & I washed & got done by 3 oclock we had a big washing, we got dinner & had it on the table by 4 o clock, Sue seems some better she set up all day again to day, I made starch & starched the babies 2 dresses Lizzie's bonnet & my white apron & then ironed one dress for the baby my apron Lizzies bonnet & some napkins Mr. Jass Baldwin ate dinner here to day, Mrs. Mattie Chiles came to see me this evening & stayed about an hour she had Ruth with her, Mrs. Morgan & Miss Annie Chiles went to Redfork to day, the water has fallen about an inch & a half

Tuesday April 7th. 1891 Cloudy & windy oh so windy cleared up in the evening but still windy, Sue went to Mrs Morgan's & stayed all day & all the rest of us went up on the ridge to the childrens speaking, it was the last day of Miss Carrie's school there & the children all had speeches & a candy stew, we all had a splendid time Mr. Jackson took Miss Fannie, Lizzie & baby & I in his dugout, & Brother Dick took Miss Josie & Asher & Harry went in a boat by themselves Mr. L. Baldwin Adie McNiel Eddie Alexander, & John Chandler were all there we composed the Watson crowd, Miss Fannie went on with Miss Carrie to Mr. Jones'[100] Sue is at Mrs. Morgans to night, Mr. Brown came here to day to board he is going to get logs for Mr. Banks at Redfork. Mr. Morgan & Mr. Alfred Stroud was up to the school to day too, but they did not stay to get any

100. Joseph H. Jones was born in 1837 in Tennessee. He was a farmer at Pea Ridge and provided the boarding place for the teacher of the Pea Ridge school.

candy I brought Sue some candy, she seems to be getting better, poor Fannie Archdale she is no better Walter Totten died to day just a year tomorrow since Willie Totten died, the water still falling

Wednesday, April 8th, 1891 Cloudy & hazy most all day & very windy, Mr. Jackson went to the ridge to day he went on to Mr. Jones & got Lizzie's valise he got back before sundown, Lizzie & I ironed to day & I did some mending Lizzie went up to see Fannie Archdale she is no better Sue came to day & Sallie Chiles came & stayed a little while, Mrs. Archdale[101] is quite sick she sent for me & I went over there & sent for Mrs. Morgan & we gave her a dose of oil & turpentine & some gum camphor, Lizzie & Mrs. Morgan are going to stay there a while to night, John Hornbuckle ate supper here to night Brother Dick went in the woods & got another ducking to day. he was with Mr. Morris, Mr. Jackson brought me a note from Miss Carrie she & Miss Fannie will be down one day next week, the water has quit running across at the wood-pile,

Thursday April 9th 1891 Cloudy some clear some & very windy, went to the store got a half gallon coaloil bottle casteroil & paid for all, also sent 20 cent to Redfork by Mr. Jackson & got .10 in writing paper & .10 in cabbage seeds, he brought Dr. Peoples back with him to see Mrs. Archdale she is very sick there is no one to set up with them to night, Mr. Jackson went to Red Fork to see Mr. Nady & he was not there to see him, but he wrote Mr. Jackson a note & he got it in the mail this evening & Mr. Nady cant help us this year & I dont know who we will get. I have been to see Mrs Archdale once to day Emmit took me & Sue went there & stayed a while, Lizzie & Mrs. Morgan & Sallie Chiles set up there all night last night, Lizzie has slept some to day I had the sick headache so bad a while to day but I am better

101. Caroline Archdale, a widow at this time, was born in 1841 in Arkansas.

97

to night I took a pill & am going to take another to morrow, the water stoped running across at the gate by ten this morning & now it has almost quit running through the yard there is land out in a good many places I have not done but little work to day, Brother Dick went in the woods to work for Mr. Brown Walter Totten was buried at the Porter ridge to day, they put his corpse in the covert house last night,

Friday, April 10th. 1891. Cloudy some clear some & windy have felt bad all day have not done much work just a little mending Lizzie washed some for the baby, Mr. Jackson went to Redfork again to day but with no better success than yesterday, Mrs. Morgan & I went to Mrs. Archdales & stayed a while she & Fannie are not much better, I went to Mrs. Morgans & ground some pepper. Lizzie is up there with her to night to help her for she took pills to day & is not very well, Sue dont seem any better she is at home to night, Lee Archdale came here & got his dinner & supper & took Fannie something to eat, Mrs. Morgan sent me a whole ham of fresh meat yesterday & we had the last of it this morning for breakfast. Brother Dick went in the woods to work for Mr. Brown again to day, the water has quit running through the yard & by to morrow we can walk to Mrs. Morgans wrote to Gert Wiggs to night & also a note to Miss Carrie,

Saturday, April 11th, 1891. Clear & bright & warmer windy but not so bad as it was yesterday, water still falling, Fannie & Lizzie walked down here this morning & I have walked up there twice to day & also walked on over to see Mrs. Archdale they are all getting better I cleaned up the dishes & stratened things about over there some, I made myself a chimise this evening, that is about all the work I have done to day Mr. Brown went home to night, Brother Dick went in the woods with him again to day, Mr. Jackson went on the ridge & Mr. Morgan went to Redfork, I sent Lizzie up to help Mrs Morgan get dinner to day. I wrote to Ella Chandler & her Ma to night also a few lines to Doc. & Lizzie wrote to Ella too, Lee Archdale was here for breakfast & supper.

Sunday, April, 12th. 1891 Clear & bright & warm, Mr. Jackson went to the ridge to make smokes for the horses & cows & Mr. Morgan went to walnut lake, Mrs. Morgan & I went to Mrs. Archdales & found her with iresypelas in her face very bad she is quite sick & Fannie is not much better, Brother Dick did not go to the ridge to day, Mrs. Morgan & I went to see Mrs. Morris a while to day & after Mr. Jackson came back he took me to see Mrs. Gifford she is sick too, so is Mr. Gifford, Lizzie is at Fannies to night, Mr. Jackson turned the chickens out of the pantry to day they have land once more

Monday, April 13th. 1891 Cloudy & drizzly & cool, Mrs. Archdale is no better she is a heap worse, Sue & I cleaned the pantry & got things mooved back in it I have had to go to Mrs. Archdales 5 or 6 times to day I dont feel very well Fannie & I have to setup there to night oh but she is so bad Brother went to the woods with Mr. Brown & they got caught in the rain, Mr. Jackson has been sick all day he is better to night Emmitt & Asher went to the ridge to day & made smokes

Tuesday, April 14th. 1891 Clear & bright & warm Mrs. Archdale died this morning at 25 minutes to one she suffered a heap before she died & talked sinsible up till about 4 or 5 hours before she died Dove got there before she died but Mr. Jimmie & the Doctor never did come. Fannie is no better, Mrs. Morgan, Mrs Newby & I Mr. Jackson Kate McNiel & Fannie Totten all set up last night & we dressed her & laid her out Charlie Totten died yesterday & was buried to day the gentlemen have to set up with the corpse to night, for Mrs. Gifford cant set up, Mrs. Morris is sick & the rest of us set up last night, Mrs. Morris had Fannie

99

Archdale taken to her house to day & she is to take care of her poor child she is no better, Mr. Jackson went to Redfork today to see about getting the coffin made & it has come & Mrs. Archdale is in it, I took a nap today but feel bad to night, Mr. Morgan got home from Walnut Lake to day I ate dinner at Fannies today so did Mrs. Chiles, Mr. Morgan ate supper here to night, I got a letter from Ella Chandler to day so did Lizzie,

Wednesday April 15th 1891. Cloudy all morning the gentlemen took Mrs. Archdale away & not a lady could go on account of the water it is falling but slow so slow, after they all went to the grave yard Mrs [illegible] & I fixed the things about in the house & I gave Bell Young the things to wash & she put them in soak, & she and Mrs. Morgan wash & I washed & got done tolerable early, & Brother Dick took me over to Mrs. [illegible] to see Fannie A. she is no better, Mr. Morgan brought me a nice lot of medicine Doc Chandler sent for Lizzie Sue & I to take when we get sick I have put my eating table back in the kitchen Mr. Brown paid his weeks board to night $2,00 two dollars & Mr. Jackson gave me a dollar, Mr. Lawrence Baldwin was here for supper he is going to work with Brother Dick this year & we are to board them Brother Charlie was here a while late this evening so was John Hornbuckle Mr. Jackson went on to Redfork from the burying

Glossary

Back bands. Web straps that go over the back of a horse to hold the harness up.

Basque. A tight-fitting bodice.

Calomel. Mercurous chloride, which was used as a cathartic.

Chicken bread. Coarse corn bread made without milk or eggs. It is used as feed for baby chickens, and is eaten by people as well when milk and eggs are in short supply.

Clabber. Thickly curdled sour milk. It tastes somewhat like yogurt and is eaten mixed with sugar.

Drench. An animal is drenched by forcing liquid down its throat.

Face cover. A cloth to put over the face of a corpse in a coffin.

Flux. Diarrhea.

Iresypelas. Misspelling of erysipelas, a streptococcus infection of the skin or mucous membrane.

Lawn dress. A sheer linen or cotton dress.

Maul. A heavy hammer used with a wedge in splitting logs.

Moss. Some species of moss is used here as a house plant.

Mother Hubbard. A full, loose dress modeled after the one worn by Mother Hubbard in the illustrations for the nursery rhyme.

Pearline. A type of thread.

Pot licker. The juice made from cooking vegetables, especially greens, in water, usually with a piece of salt pork thrown in for seasoning.

Souce. Souse, or head cheese.

Vinegar pie. A pie made with vinegar instead of lemons. Lemons were a luxury in Watson in 1890.

Water table. Probably a table for water buckets to stand on.

Bibliography

Unpublished Sources

Jones Family Papers, in the hands of Mrs. Pauline Lloyd at Watson, Arkansas.

History of Watson, Arkansas, compiled by Judge Jim Merritt at McGehee, Arkansas.

Stillwell Family Papers, in the hands of Mrs. Virginia Sue Meade at Pine Bluff, Arkansas.

Tax Records, Desha County, Arkansas. Vol. 1886 and vol. 1890, Desha County Courthouse, Arkansas City, Arkansas.

Published Sources

The Biographical and Historical Memoirs of Southern Arkansas. Chicago, Nashville, and St. Louis: Goodspeed, 1890.

Conklin, Henry. *Through Poverty's Vale*, ed. Wendell Tripp. Syracuse: Syracuse University Press, 1974.

Emerson, Mrs. L. A. "History of Railroads in Arkansas and Desha County." *Programs of the Desha County Historical Society* 5 (Summer 1979): 23–29.

French, Marilyn. *The Women's Room.* New York: Summit, 1977.

Hempstead, Fay. *A Pictorial History of Arkansas.* St. Louis and New York: Thompson, 1890.

"Population of Arkansas by Minor Civil Divisions." *Census Bulletin* no. 112. Washington, D.C.: Department of the Interior, 1890.

Simkins, Francis Butler. *The South.* New York: Alfred A. Knopf, 1947.

Stanley, Henry M. *Autobiography.* Boston and New York: Houghton and Mifflin, 1909.

Thane, Henry. "Early Days in Southeast Arkansas." *Programs of the Desha County Historical Society* 3 (Spring 1977): 28–41.

Thanet, Octave. "Town Life in Arkansas." *Atlantic Monthly* 68 (September 1891): 332–40.

United States Census for 1880.

United States Census for 1900.

Index

Agee, James, 3
Alexander, Eddie, 82, 93, 94, 96
Allen, Mr., 70–73, 79, 80, 84, 91
Archdale, Bill, 88, 90–92
Archdale, Fannie, 57, 91, 92, 97–100
Archdale, Lee, 88, 90–92, 98, 99
Archdale, Mrs., 64, 88, 90–93, 97–100
Arkansas City Journal, 6, 33, 54, 67
Ashley, Mollie, 78, 89
Atkins, Mr., 17, 18, 53, 54, 58
Atkins, Mrs., 88
Austin, Dr., 75

Baldwin, Jass, 93, 96
Baldwin, Lawrence, 79, 80, 92, 96, 100
Bankhead, Talullah, 90
Bankhead, William B., 90n
Banks, Mr., 96
Beadle, Charles, 56
Benson, Anna, 61, 74, 88
Black, Lucinda, 54, 67, 83, 85, 89
Blidenburg, Mrs., 84
Branch, Emma, 78
Branch, Francine, 50, 52
Brogan, Mrs., 64
Brooks, Tony, 75
Brother Jim, 37, 38, 40, 42, 45, 47, 66, 67, 72
Brown, Mr., 67, 72, 98, 99, 100
Brown, Mrs., 81
Burnett, Elizabeth Coose (Cousin Lizzie), 29, 37
Burnett, William H., Jr., 14, 28, 30, 46, 88, 89, 95

Caldwell, Mamie (Cousin Mamie), 17, 31, 36, 59, 72, 77, 85
Caldwell, Mollie, 77n, 85
Caulk, Mrs. Benjamin, 41, 47, 53, 65
Chandler, Earl J., 26n
Chandler, Ella, 18, 27, 33–35, 39, 40, 42–44, 47, 48, 57, 59, 65, 72, 74, 80, 93, 98, 100
Chandler, James, 26n
Chandler, John, 96
Chandler, Dr. Thomas Charles, 16, 17, 26, 30, 41, 50, 56, 59–62, 70, 73, 80, 84, 87, 93, 99, 100
Chandler, Mrs. Thomas Charles, 16, 17, 29, 31–33, 36, 40, 41, 43, 47, 48, 50, 52–56, 58, 60–62, 80, 81, 88
Cheatham, Caroline, 12, 30, 55, 57, 60–62, 77, 83, 88
Cheatham, John W., 12, 88, 94
Cheatham, Katie, 55, 57, 88
Chestine, Mr., 77
Chestine, Mrs., 78, 88
Chiles, Annie, 64, 74, 80–83, 93, 95, 96
Chiles, Mattie (Mrs. Chiles), 36, 47, 58, 92, 96, 100
Chiles, Mayson, 18, 69, 70, 88
Chiles, Ruth, 96
Chiles, Sallie, 97
Coalman, Caroline, 9, 63n, 65, 68, 74
Coalman, Prince, 63
Coalman, Rosa, 9, 56
Cobb, Louisa, 69
Combs, Col., 80
Conklin, Henry, 21
Coopwood, Benjamin J., 50, 64, 94
Coopwood, Lula, 86, 87
Coopwood, Mrs. Benjamin J., 48, 51, 64, 65
Coose, James Conner, 11

Davis, Ella, 68
Davis, Emeline, 57, 58, 61, 62, 66, 69
Dyer, Mr., 18, 66, 69, 70
Dyer, Mrs., 25, 29, 31, 37, 39, 45, 47, 48, 53, 67

Edington, Alfie, 40, 42, 49, 51, 54, 57, 64, 69

Edington, Lizzie, 40
Emerick, Mr., 63
Emmit, Will, 10, 18, 43, 59, 61–63, 66–69, 71, 72, 74–78, 84, 87, 97, 99

Faulkner, William, 2
Ferguson, John R., 92
Frazier, Thomas R., 1
French, Marilyn, 15

Gates, Mrs., 32
Gifford, Annie (Mrs. Gifford), 25, 31, 46, 57, 60, 65, 66, 73, 74, 76, 79, 86, 94, 99
Gifford, Josie, 25, 31, 47, 54, 66, 80, 91, 93, 96
Gifford, Lula, 25, 68, 71, 77
Gifford, Mollie, 56
Gifford, Mr., 73
Gifford, Tom, 56
Goodman, Mike, 34
Gordan, Ed, 25, 32, 36, 38, 39, 40, 41, 43–45, 54, 57, 62
Graves, John B., 11

Hall, Mrs., 32, 36
Hazel, Alex, 18, 40, 50, 53, 54, 62, 66, 72, 74
Hazel, Elie, 48
Henry, John, 68
Hicks, Charlie, 33
Hickson, Lee, 25, 27
Hines, Frances, 9, 33, 55, 56, 59, 63, 68, 74, 89
Hornbuckle, John, 39, 51, 66, 70, 92, 93, 96, 97, 100
Hornbuckle, Martha, 51, 66, 67, 70, 85
Hornbuckle, Sam, 66
Howard, Bell, 52
Howell, Ida, 62
Howell, Iola, 45
Howell, Ione, 52, 76
Howell, James S., 27
Howell, Lon, 43, 44, 55, 74
Howell, Mrs. James, 17, 44, 45, 48, 50, 56, 58, 73, 76, 77
Hudson: Abraham, Tabitha, Nannie, 11
Hundley, Betty, 42, 66–69, 71

Hundley, Edgar, 42n
Hundley, Frank, 42
Hurd, Fannie, 59

Irby, Albert Zedekiah, 60
Irby, Hattie, 42n

Jackson, Caroline, 11
Jackson, Carrie M., 12
Jackson, Charles, 51, 58, 66, 67, 70, 72, 74, 75, 100
Jackson, Richard (Brother Dick), 18, 39–60, 62, 65–77, 82–85, 87–96, 98–100
Jackson, Stonewall J. (Davie Samuel), 12, 61, 64, 78, 89–91
Jackson, William T., 10, 11, 14, 16; mentioned throughout diary
Jones, Joseph H., 96, 97
Jones, Sallie, 6

Lee, Billie (William), 62, 72, 82
Lee, Victoria, 66, 68–70, 76, 80, 81, 83, 88, 95
Lowen, Charles H., 74

McEncro, Myrtle, 55
McGehee Times, 4
McNiel, Adie, 47, 83, 86, 96
McNiel, Alfie, 41, 42, 45
McNiel, Cam, 47, 79, 80, 87
McNiel, Kate, 46, 47, 63, 65, 66, 69, 82, 99
McNiel, Mary (Mrs. McNiel), 41, 82, 83, 95
Malaria, 7
Malpass, Charles S., 95
Malpass, Minnerva, 10, 37
Mann, Eddie, 65, 69, 72, 84
Mask, Jane, 29, 51, 62, 71, 93
Mayson, Mollie, 73, 74
Meade, Virginia Sue, 12
Medford, 4
Miller, Sister Bettie, 25, 27, 57, 64
Morgan, Asher, 15n, 30, 33, 34, 36, 41, 43, 46, 48, 49, 54, 57, 58, 62, 65, 67, 69, 79, 84, 85, 87, 95, 96, 99
Morgan, Charles (Mr. Morgan), 18, 19, 27, 30, 34, 35, 40, 41, 43, 48, 50, 52–54, 57, 59, 60,

62, 69, 72, 75, 76, 79, 84, 85, 87–89, 93–96, 100
Morgan, Fannie (Mrs. Morgan), 10, 11, 15–17; mentioned throughout diary
Morgan, Harry, 29, 30, 39, 43, 48, 54, 65, 73, 79, 84, 87, 95, 96
Morgan, Willie, 29, 33, 34, 40, 48, 54, 73, 76, 77, 79, 80
Morris, Mr., 47, 58, 72, 84, 85, 87, 89, 90, 92, 93, 97
Morris, Mrs., 67, 85, 99

Nady, Frank, 11, 82, 94, 97
Nady, Mrs. Frank, 79
Newby, Bettie, 74, 76, 77, 82, 99
Newby, Dove, 75

Osburn, Jane, 55, 59
Osburn, Nick, 51, 55n
Outlaw, Ben, 58, 66
Owen, Carrie, 17, 53, 57, 58, 62–73, 76–83, 89–91, 93, 94, 96–98
Owen, Fannie, 6, 10, 17, 45, 63, 64, 78–88, 90, 92–97

Peoples, Eddie (J. Edward), 65
Peoples, Dr. S. J., 40, 93, 97
Pindall, Judge Xenophon J., 41, 68, 69, 80, 83
Pindall, Xenophon O., 41n
Pointer, Mr., 85
Porter, Mrs., 76

Railroads: Little Rock, Mississippi River and Texas, 5; Little Rock, Pine Bluff and New Orleans, 4; Missouri Pacific, 20; North Memphis, Helena and Louisiana, 42
Reddick, Alice, 33
Reed, Henry, 52, 53, 59
Reed, Lula, 66
Ryan, Van R. (Cousin Van), 53, 57, 59, 60, 85

Sain, Bettie, 48
Sample, Mr., 68
Scales, Mr., 91
Simmons, Mrs., 47

Sims, Mary, 85
Sledge, Ada, 90n
Sledge, Eugenia, 90n
Sledge, Tom, 90
Smith, Fannie, 42
Smith, Mrs., 44, 61, 63, 76, 85
Smith, Polly, 42
Smithee, Nellie, 10, 16–18, 27, 29–31, 33, 35, 38, 40, 42, 44, 45, 47, 48, 50–55, 58, 61, 67, 69, 70, 74, 77, 79, 81, 82, 92
Stamp, Elizabeth, 47, 56
Stanley, Sir Henry Morton, 8, 56
Stillwell, Asher C., 11, 12, 14, 16, 38, 57
Stillwell, Dennie, 45, 47
Stillwell, Etta Elizabeth (Lizzie), 11, 17–20; mentioned throughout diary
Stillwell, Mary Sue, 11, 16–20; mentioned throughout diary
Stillwell, William A., 11
Stroud, Alfred, 49, 90, 96
Stroud, Hadley, 34n
Stroud, Maggie, 34, 38, 56, 69, 71
Stroud, Marshall, 75, 77, 85, 89
Stroud, Mat, 73–75
Stroud, May, 42, 57, 60, 61

Thane, Henry, 4
Thanet, Octave, 6
Thomas, Mollie Gifford, 56
Tillar, 6
Totten, Fannie, 83, 99
Totten, Walter, 47, 48, 50, 83, 97, 98
Totten, Willie, 97
Trippe, 6
Turner, Chaney, 9, 51, 53, 55–62, 67–69
Typhoid fever, 7

Watkins, Frank, 79–81, 92
Watkins, Molly, 89
Watkins, Sallie, 36, 44, 45, 63, 64, 67, 68, 76, 79, 80, 85, 86, 95
Watkins, William T. (Will), 40, 45, 46, 63
Watson, Jake, 59
Watson, L. W., 4
Watson, Mrs., 55, 56, 67

Watson, Susan, 33, 34
Welty, Eudora, 2
White, Blanche, 41–45, 60, 75
Wiggs, Gert, 98
Wiggs, Mr., 66
Williams, Mary, 42, 43, 49, 55
Willis, Pete, 33, 35, 39, 47, 94

Wilson, Sallie, 45, 53, 54, 62
Winn, Mr., 77
Winn, Mrs., 44
Winters, Mrs., 36

Young, Bell, 54, 71, 87, 89, 100